RAJASTHAN TRAVEL GUIDE 2024

Veer James

All rights reserved. No part of this publication may be reproduced, distributed, or transmitted in any means, including photocopying, recording, or other electronic or mechanical methods, without the prior written permission of the publisher.

Copyright© **Veer James** 2024

Rajasthan The Land of Kings 9

Chapter 1 11

Top Attractions 11

Best museums in Rajasthan 26

Best festivals in Rajasthan 32

Chapter 2 35

Planning Your Trip... 35

Visa and passport requirements of Rajasthan 35

Best time to visit Rajasthan 41

Transportation options to Rajasthan 47

Chapter 3 51

Getting Around the City 51

Public Transportation Tips in Rajasthan 56

Traveling to Rajasthan Nearby Cities 60

Chapter 4 77

Travel essentials in Rajasthan 77

Things to know before you travel to Rajasthan 83

Local customs and etiquette in Rajasthan 85

Safety and emergency information of Rajasthan 89

Chapter 5 93

Where To Stay in Rajasthan 93

Accommodation options in Rajasthan 93

Hotels And Resorts 96

   Luxury Accommodations in Rajasthan 96

   Mid-Range Options in Rajasthan 99

   Budget-Friendly Stays in Rajasthan 101

Alternative Lodging 104

   Bed and Breakfasts in Rajasthan 104

   Vacation Rentals in Rajasthan 106

Things to consider when deciding where to stay in Rajasthan 109

Chapter 6 115

Practical Tips 115

Budget 115

Language and communication of Rajasthan 118

Arts and Theaters in Rajasthan 122

Chapter 7 125

Cultural Experiences 125

Best Traditional Foods to Try in Rajasthan 125

Best restaurants in Rajasthan 129

Top shopping areas in Rajasthan 134

Chapter 8 139

Family Activities 139
   Couples In Rajasthan 139
   Rajasthan With kids 143

Chapter 9 149

Outdoor Activities 149
   Hiking and Nature Trails 149
   Water-based Activities 150
   Parks and Recreation Areas 152
   Cycling and Biking 153

Chapter 10 157
   Nightlife in Rajasthan 157

Conclusion And Further Resources for Planning Your Trip to Rajasthan 159

Appendices 163
   Glossary of Local Phrases in Rajasthan 163
   Useful Contacts 168
   Sample Itineraries 172
      Sample Itinerary 1: "Golden Triangle and Beyond" 172
      Sample Itinerary 2: "Desert Delight" 174
      Sample Itinerary 3: "Cultural Extravaganza" 175
   Packing Checklist 178

Safe Travels!..181

Rajasthan The Land of Kings

Rajasthan, the largest state in India, is a vibrant tapestry of history, culture, and architectural marvels. Nestled in the northwestern part of the country, the state is renowned for its majestic cities that reflect the opulence and grandeur of its past rulers. Each city within Rajasthan boasts a unique identity, contributing to the rich heritage of the region.

The capital city, Jaipur, often referred to as the "Pink City," stands as a testament to the visionary planning of Maharaja Sawai Jai Singh II. Its distinct pink-colored buildings, designed to mimic the architecture of Mughal cities, create a captivating urban landscape. Jaipur serves as a hub for traditional arts and crafts, with bustling bazaars and vibrant markets showcasing the skilled craftsmanship of the region.

Jodhpur, known as the "Blue City," is a captivating blend of history and modernity. Dominated by the imposing Mehrangarh Fort, the city's skyline is punctuated by indigo-hued houses that earned it the moniker. The winding streets of the old town, with its vibrant markets and bustling squares, provide a glimpse into the daily lives of the locals.

Udaipur, often hailed as the "City of Lakes," exudes a romantic charm with its picturesque water bodies and stunning palaces. The serene Lake Pichola and Fateh Sagar Lake are iconic landmarks, surrounded by palatial structures like the City Palace and Jag Mandir. Udaipur's well-preserved architecture and tranquil ambiance make it a popular destination for those seeking a romantic and leisurely escape.

The golden-hued city of Jaisalmer, situated amidst the Thar Desert, is a mesmerizing oasis of sandstone architecture. The Jaisalmer Fort, a UNESCO World Heritage Site, stands proudly against the arid landscape, reflecting the region's military and trading history. The intricate carvings on the havelis (mansions) and the vibrant markets add to the city's unique character.

Bikaner, founded by Rao Bika in the 15th century, is renowned for its imposing forts and vibrant festivals. The Junagarh Fort, an architectural marvel, showcases a fusion of Rajput and Mughal styles. Bikaner's camel breeding farm, Karni Mata Temple with its resident rat population, and the Laxmi Niwas Palace contribute to the city's diverse attractions.

Known as the "Land of Kings," Rajasthan is dotted with numerous lesser-known cities and towns, each with its own distinct flavor.

Rajasthan is more than just a city; it is a captivating tapestry of contrasts that weaves together the threads of tradition and modernity.

Chapter 1

Top Attractions

Amber Fort (Amer Fort), Jaipur: Perched on a hill overlooking Maota Lake, Amber Fort is a stunning blend of Rajput and Mughal architecture. The fort's intricate design, with its elaborate palaces, courtyards, and the Sheesh Mahal (Mirror Palace), reflects the opulence of the Rajput rulers.

City Palace, Jaipur: Located in the heart of Jaipur, the City Palace is a magnificent complex of courtyards, gardens, and buildings. A seamless fusion of Rajasthani and Mughal architecture, the palace houses museums showcasing royal artifacts, textiles, and art.

Hawa Mahal, Jaipur: The iconic "Palace of the Winds" is a unique five-story structure with intricately designed windows, allowing the royal women to observe street festivities without being seen. Its pink sandstone façade is an epitome of Jaipur's architectural beauty.

Jantar Mantar, Jaipur: A UNESCO World Heritage Site, Jantar Mantar is an astronomical observatory built by Maharaja Sawai Jai Singh II. The complex houses a collection of architectural instruments, each serving a specific astronomical purpose.

Mehrangarh Fort, Jodhpur: Perched on a rocky hill, Mehrangarh Fort dominates the skyline of Jodhpur. The fort's massive walls house palaces with intricately carved panels, expansive courtyards, and a museum displaying artifacts, weapons, and textiles.

Udaipur City Palace: Set on the banks of Lake Pichola, the Udaipur City Palace is a majestic complex of palaces, courtyards, and gardens. The panoramic views of the lake and the city make it a romantic and picturesque destination.

Lake Palace, Udaipur: Floating on Lake Pichola, the Lake Palace is an architectural marvel that served as the summer palace for the royal family. The palace's white marble façade against the backdrop of the lake creates a mesmerizing sight.

Jag Mandir, Udaipur: Also known as the "Lake Garden Palace," Jag Mandir is an island palace in Lake Pichola. Its impressive architecture, including carved elephants and chhatri (cenotaphs), makes it a must-visit attraction.

Jaisalmer Fort: A UNESCO World Heritage Site, Jaisalmer Fort stands as a golden sentinel in the Thar Desert. The fort's intricate architecture, narrow alleys, and ancient havelis transport visitors to a bygone era.

Patwon Ki Haveli, Jaisalmer: A cluster of five havelis, Patwon Ki Haveli is a marvel of architecture adorned with intricate carvings, arches, and balconies. Each haveli tells a unique story of the wealthy merchant families that once resided there.

Junagarh Fort, Bikaner: Built by Raja Rai Singh, Junagarh Fort is an imposing structure that showcases a harmonious blend of Rajput and Mughal architecture. The fort houses palaces, temples, and a museum displaying artifacts from different eras.

City Palace, Alwar: Alwar's City Palace is a captivating blend of Mughal and Rajput architecture. The palace houses a museum with a remarkable collection of artifacts, including royal costumes, weapons, and paintings.

Ranthambore National Park: Renowned for its tiger population, Ranthambore National Park offers a thrilling wildlife experience. The park's landscape, dotted with lakes and ancient forts, provides a picturesque backdrop for safari adventures.

Chittorgarh Fort: One of the largest forts in India, Chittorgarh Fort narrates tales of valor and sacrifice. Its massive gates, towers, and reservoirs make it a monumental representation of Rajput architecture.

Sariska Tiger Reserve: Sariska Tiger Reserve, nestled in the Aravalli Range, is a haven for wildlife enthusiasts. Apart from tigers, the reserve is home to a variety of fauna, including leopards, sambar deer, and numerous bird species.

Best museums in Rajasthan

Here, we explore the best museums that showcase the historical, artistic, and cultural treasures of Rajasthan.

1. Albert Hall Museum, Jaipur: Located in the heart of Jaipur, the Albert Hall Museum is a splendid example of Indo-Saracenic architecture. Built to commemorate the visit of Prince Albert, it houses an extensive collection of artifacts, including sculptures, paintings, decorative arts, and an Egyptian mummy. The museum's grand architecture and diverse exhibits make it a must-visit for history and art enthusiasts.

2. City Palace Museum, Udaipur: Nestled within the magnificent City Palace complex in Udaipur, this museum offers a rich collection of royal artifacts. From ornate clothing and accessories worn by the Mewar rulers to intricate miniature paintings and antique weaponry, the museum provides a comprehensive insight into the opulent lifestyle of the Maharanas.

3. Mehrangarh Museum, Jodhpur: Situated within the Mehrangarh Fort, this museum is a treasure trove of artifacts showcasing the military history and cultural heritage of Marwar. The exhibits include royal palanquins, arms, costumes, and an impressive collection of miniature paintings. The museum's location within the formidable fort adds to the overall experience.

4. Hawa Mahal Museum, Jaipur: Housed within the iconic Hawa Mahal, this museum offers a fascinating journey into the history and architecture of the "Palace of the Winds." The exhibits include artifacts, photographs, and models that shed light on the construction and purpose of this unique structure. Visitors can gain insights into the lifestyle of the royal women who once used the Hawa Mahal.

5. Maharaja Sawai Man Singh II Museum, Jaipur: Situated within the City Palace complex in Jaipur, this museum is dedicated to Maharaja Sawai Man Singh II. It showcases his personal belongings, including textiles, artifacts, and photographs, providing a glimpse into the life of this influential ruler. The museum also houses an impressive collection of weaponry and royal memorabilia.

6. Junagarh Fort Museum, Bikaner: The museum within Junagarh Fort in Bikaner is a repository of historical artifacts spanning several centuries. From intricate jewelry and costumes to antique firearms and manuscripts, the exhibits offer a comprehensive overview of the cultural and military history of the region. The museum's architecture, within the confines of the impressive fort, adds to its allure.

7. Umaid Bhawan Palace Museum, Jodhpur: Situated within the lavish Umaid Bhawan Palace, this museum showcases the royal lifestyle of the Jodhpur rulers. The exhibits include vintage cars, artifacts, and memorabilia from the bygone era. The opulent surroundings of the palace enhance the regal ambiance of the museum.

8. City Palace Museum, Alwar: Alwar's City Palace houses a museum that exhibits a diverse range of artifacts, including royal costumes, antique weapons, and intricately crafted jewelry. The museum provides a comprehensive understanding of the history and culture of Alwar.

9. Sardar Government Museum, Jodhpur: Founded in 1909, the Sardar Government Museum in Jodhpur is dedicated to preserving the artistic and cultural heritage of Rajasthan. It houses a rich collection of paintings, sculptures, arms, and manuscripts. The museum's emphasis on regional art makes it a valuable resource for those interested in the artistic traditions of Rajasthan.

10. Bagore Ki Haveli Museum, Udaipur: Located on the banks of Lake Pichola, Bagore Ki Haveli is a historic mansion that has been transformed into a museum. The exhibits include traditional Mewar paintings, costumes, and artifacts, offering a glimpse into the cultural heritage of Udaipur. The museum also hosts cultural performances, adding an immersive experience for visitors.

11. Rajasthan State Archives, Bikaner: For those interested in delving into historical documents and records, the Rajasthan State Archives in Bikaner is a significant repository. It houses a vast collection of manuscripts, official records, and historical documents, providing valuable insights into the administrative and cultural history of the region.

12. Anokhi Museum of Hand Printing, Jaipur: Dedicated to the traditional art of hand block printing, the Anokhi Museum in Jaipur showcases the history and techniques of this ancient craft. The exhibits include a diverse range of textiles, block prints, and tools, offering visitors a deeper understanding of the rich textile heritage of Rajasthan.

13. Maharana Pratap Museum, Udaipur: Located within the City Palace complex in Udaipur, this museum is dedicated to the legendary Rajput warrior Maharana Pratap. The exhibits include his weapons, armor, and personal belongings, allowing visitors to connect with the heroic tales of Rajasthan's past.

14. Archaeological Museum, Amer: Situated near the Amer Fort in Jaipur, the Archaeological Museum houses a collection of artifacts dating back to the prehistoric and medieval periods. The exhibits include sculptures, coins, and pottery, providing a glimpse into the archaeological heritage of the region.

15. Government Museum, Kota: Kota's Government Museum is a cultural hub that displays artifacts related to the history, art, and crafts of the region. The museum's diverse exhibits include sculptures, paintings, and traditional handicrafts, making it a comprehensive repository of Kota's cultural wealth.

16. Prachina Museum, Bikaner: Dedicated to preserving the cultural heritage of Bikaner, the Prachina Museum showcases traditional costumes, textiles, and artifacts. The museum's exhibits provide insights into the social and cultural life of the region.

17. Raja Dinkar Kelkar Museum, Jaipur: Founded by Dr. Dinkar G. Kelkar, this museum in Jaipur is a treasure trove of artifacts collected from different parts of India. The exhibits include sculptures, jewelry, musical instruments, and household items, offering a diverse representation of Indian art and culture.

18. Desert Culture Centre and Museum, Jaisalmer: Located in Jaisalmer, this museum is dedicated to showcasing the cultural and historical heritage of the Thar Desert. The exhibits include traditional costumes, artifacts, and musical instruments, providing visitors with a deeper understanding of the desert lifestyle.

19. Rajputana Museum, Jaisalmer: Housed within the Jaisalmer Fort, the Rajputana Museum exhibits artifacts related to the royal history of the Rajput rulers. The displays include weapons, manuscripts, and decorative arts, offering a comprehensive overview of Jaisalmer's regal past.

20. Maharana Kumbha Sangeet Kala Trust, Udaipur: For enthusiasts of classical music and performing arts, the Maharana Kumbha Sangeet Kala Trust in Udaipur is a cultural gem. The trust organizes events, exhibitions, and performances to promote and preserve the traditional music and arts of Rajasthan.

Best festivals in Rajasthan

Let's delve into some of the best festivals in Rajasthan.

Pushkar Camel Fair: The Pushkar Camel Fair is one of the most iconic and unique festivals in Rajasthan. Held annually in the holy town of Pushkar, it is a vibrant amalgamation of a traditional livestock fair and a religious gathering. The fair attracts thousands of camels, cattle, and traders from across the region. Pilgrims also gather to take a dip in the sacred Pushkar Lake during this time. The highlight of the festival is the camel beauty contest, where these majestic animals are adorned with colorful attire and intricate jewelry, creating a mesmerizing spectacle.

Holi – The Festival of Colors: Holi, the festival of colors, is a joyous celebration that marks the arrival of spring. In Rajasthan, Holi is celebrated with exuberance and a riot of colors. Locals and tourists alike come together to play with gulal (colored powder), dance to traditional folk music, and indulge in festive sweets. The cities, towns, and villages of Rajasthan become a kaleidoscope of hues during this lively festival.

Kite Festival (Makar Sankranti): Makar Sankranti, marking the transition of the sun into the zodiac sign of Capricorn, is celebrated with great fervor in Rajasthan as the Kite Festival. The skies of cities like Jaipur and

Jodhpur come alive with colorful kites of all shapes and sizes. The friendly kite-flying competitions, traditional sweets, and cultural performances make it a joyous and visually stunning celebration.

Nagaur Fair: The Nagaur Fair is one of the largest cattle fairs in Rajasthan, attracting traders and livestock owners from different parts of the country. The fair is a vibrant spectacle of color, with cattle, camels, and horses being bought and sold. Traditional music and dance performances, camel races, and various competitions add to the festive atmosphere.

Rajasthan International Film Festival (RIFF): While not a traditional cultural festival, RIFF is a significant event that brings together filmmakers, actors, and film enthusiasts from around the world. Held in Jaipur, RIFF showcases a diverse range of films, documentaries, and short films, providing a platform for cultural exchange and appreciation of cinema.

Summer Festival, Mount Abu: As the only hill station in Rajasthan, Mount Abu hosts the Summer Festival to provide respite from the scorching heat. The festival includes a boat race on Nakki Lake, traditional folk performances, and a showcase of the region's art and craft. The pleasant weather and cultural events make it a popular festival in the state.

Shilpgram Utsav, Udaipur: Shilpgram Utsav is a celebration of traditional arts and crafts held in the Shilpgram village near Udaipur. The festival showcases the diverse handicrafts, textiles, and art forms of Rajasthan, providing a platform for local artisans to exhibit their skills. Cultural performances, workshops, and exhibitions add to the festive atmosphere.

The festivals of Rajasthan are a vibrant expression of the state's rich cultural heritage, religious diversity, and the joyful spirit of its people.

Chapter 2

Planning Your Trip

Visa and passport requirements of Rajasthan

Visa Requirements:

1. **Tourist Visa:**
   - Most foreign nationals planning to visit Rajasthan, India, for tourism purposes require a tourist visa.
   - Tourist visas are usually issued for a specific duration, and applicants need to apply in advance before their intended travel dates.

2. **E-Visa:**
   - India offers an E-Visa facility for citizens of many countries, allowing them to apply for a visa online.
   - E-Visas are available for purposes such as tourism, business, and medical visits.
   - Applicants need to apply for an E-Visa through the official website of the Indian government,

providing the required information and documents.

3. **Visa on Arrival:**
    - As of my last update, India provides a Visa on Arrival facility for citizens of certain countries. However, this process may be subject to change, and it's crucial to verify the current status before planning travel.
    - Travelers eligible for Visa on Arrival should check the specific requirements and conditions for obtaining it.

4. **Visa Application Process:**
    - The application process generally involves submitting the required documents, including a valid passport, passport-sized photographs, and a completed application form.
    - It's advisable to apply for a visa well in advance of the planned travel date, as processing times may vary.

5. **Visa Extension:**
   - Tourists who wish to extend their stay in India beyond the validity of their visa may need to apply for an extension.
   - Extensions are subject to approval, and travelers should be aware of the rules and regulations regarding visa extensions.

Passport Requirements:

1. **Valid Passport:**
   - Travelers visiting Rajasthan, India, must possess a valid passport. The passport should be valid for at least six months beyond the intended period of stay in the country.

2. **Passport Size Photographs:**
   - Applicants are generally required to submit recent passport-sized photographs along with their visa application.

3. **Pages in Passport:**
   - It's recommended to have several blank pages in the passport for visa stamps upon entry and exit.

4. **Passport Renewal:**
    - Travelers with passports nearing expiration should consider renewing their passports well in advance to avoid complications during the visa application process.

5. **Lost or Stolen Passport:**
    - In the unfortunate event of a lost or stolen passport, travelers should report the incident to the local police and contact their embassy or consulate for guidance on obtaining a new travel document.

6. **Passport Copies:**
    - It's advisable to carry photocopies of the passport, including the main information page and the visa page, while exploring Rajasthan. These copies can be helpful in case the original documents are lost or misplaced.

Additional Tips:

1. **Consular Services:**
    - International tourists should be aware of the location and contact information of their country's embassy or consulate in India. These offices can

provide assistance in case of emergencies or other issues.

2. **Travel Insurance:**
   - Having comprehensive travel insurance is advisable for all international travelers. It can cover medical emergencies, trip cancellations, lost baggage, and other unforeseen circumstances.

3. **Entry Requirements:**
   - Travelers should check specific entry requirements for India, such as any restrictions or health-related protocols. These requirements can vary, especially during extraordinary circumstances like health crises.

4. **Registration with FRRO:**
   - Foreign nationals who plan to stay in India for an extended period may be required to register with the Foreigners Regional Registration Office (FRRO) within a specified time frame after arrival.

5. **Check for Updates:**
   - Visa and passport requirements can change, and it's crucial to stay informed about any updates or changes in regulations. Travelers should regularly check the official website of the Indian government

or contact the nearest embassy or consulate for the latest information.

international tourists planning to visit Rajasthan, India, must ensure they have the appropriate visa and a valid passport.

Best time to visit Rajasthan

Here, we explore the different seasons and factors that can influence the ideal time to explore this enchanting region.

1. Winter (October to March): The winter months, spanning from October to March, are widely considered the best time to visit Rajasthan. The weather during this period is characterized by cool and pleasant temperatures, making it ideal for exploring the historical monuments, palaces, and vibrant markets that define Rajasthan's charm.

- **Temperature:**
  - Daytime temperatures range from 15°C to 25°C (59°F to 77°F), offering a comfortable and enjoyable climate.
  - Nights can be chilly, with temperatures ranging from 5°C to 15°C (41°F to 59°F).
- **Festivals and Events:**
  - The winter season coincides with several cultural festivals in Rajasthan, including the Pushkar Camel Fair in November and the vibrant celebrations of Diwali, Navratri, and Holi.

- The Desert Festival in Jaisalmer, held in January or February, is a highlight, showcasing the region's traditional music, dance, and cultural heritage.

- **Wildlife Safari:**
  - Winter is an excellent time for wildlife enthusiasts to visit Rajasthan's national parks, such as Ranthambore and Sariska. The dry and cooler weather increases the chances of spotting diverse wildlife, including tigers.

- **Outdoor Activities:**
  - Travelers can comfortably explore outdoor attractions, such as the Thar Desert, without the extreme heat of summer.

- **Cultural Exploration:**
  - The winter season allows for comfortable exploration of the numerous palaces, forts, and historical sites across Rajasthan, including the City Palace in Jaipur and Mehrangarh Fort in Jodhpur.

2. Spring (March to June): Spring in Rajasthan, particularly March and April, offers a transitional period between winter and the scorching summer. While March still provides pleasant weather for travel, temperatures gradually begin to rise as summer approaches.

- **Temperature:**
    - Daytime temperatures in March and April range from 25°C to 35°C (77°F to 95°F).
    - As April progresses into May and June, temperatures can soar, exceeding 40°C (104°F) in some regions.
- **Festivals and Events:**
    - The festival of Gangaur, celebrated in March or April, is a significant cultural event, particularly in Udaipur, where processions and traditional rituals take place.
- **Floral Blooms:**
    - Spring sees the blossoming of vibrant flowers, adding color to the landscapes. The gardens of cities like Jaipur and Udaipur are particularly beautiful during this time.
- **Early Summer Wildlife Viewing:**
    - In early spring, wildlife enthusiasts can still enjoy visiting national parks for wildlife viewing before the temperatures become too extreme.

3. Summer (June to September): Summer in Rajasthan is characterized by scorching temperatures, especially in June and July. The period from June to September also brings the monsoon season, which brings relief from the heat but can impact travel plans due to heavy rainfall.

- **Temperature:**
    - Daytime temperatures can exceed 40°C (104°F) in June and July.
    - Monsoon begins in July, bringing relief with slightly lower temperatures but increased humidity.

- **Festivals and Events:**
    - While major festivals are not as prevalent during the summer, the Teej festival in August is celebrated with fervor, particularly in Jaipur.

- **Monsoon Landscapes:**
    - The monsoon season transforms the arid landscapes of Rajasthan into lush greenery. The Aravalli Hills and surrounding areas become particularly scenic.

- **Wildlife and Bird Watching:**
    - Monsoon is a great time for birdwatching as the rain brings out a variety of avian species. Keoladeo

National Park in Bharatpur is renowned for birdwatching during this period.

- **Cultural Experience:**
  - Some travelers might appreciate the unique charm of experiencing Rajasthan during the monsoon, with fewer crowds and a different atmosphere.

4. **Post-Monsoon/Early Autumn (September to October):** As the monsoon season concludes in September, the landscape begins to transform again, making it an interesting time to visit Rajasthan. Early autumn provides a brief window before the winter season, offering a blend of rejuvenated landscapes and comfortable temperatures.

- **Temperature:**
  - Daytime temperatures range from 25°C to 35°C (77°F to 95°F), making it a pleasant time for outdoor activities.
  - Nights are cooler compared to summer.

- **Post-Monsoon Landscapes:**
  - The post-monsoon period sees the continuation of greenery, with landscapes still lush from the recent rainfall.

- **Cultural and Festive Atmosphere:**
    - Festivals like Navratri, celebrated in September or October, and Dussehra bring a vibrant and festive atmosphere to Rajasthan.
- **Wildlife Viewing:**
    - The post-monsoon period is suitable for wildlife viewing in national parks, with vegetation remaining lush and water sources replenished.

The best time to visit Rajasthan depends on individual preferences, the desired experiences, and the tolerance for different weather conditions.

Transportation options to Rajasthan

Let's outline the various transportation options available for travelers arriving in Rajasthan from other countries.

1. International Flights:

Arriving at Major Airports: Rajasthan is well-connected to major international airports, with several cities serving as gateways for travelers. The primary international airports in Rajasthan are:

- **Jaipur International Airport (JAI):** Located in the capital city of Jaipur, this airport is the busiest in the state, handling numerous international flights.

- **Jodhpur Airport (JDH):** Jodhpur's airport also serves as an international gateway, providing connectivity to several countries.

- **Udaipur Maharana Pratap Airport (UDR):** Udaipur's airport caters to international travelers, offering a convenient entry point to explore the city and nearby destinations.

International Airlines: Numerous international airlines operate flights to Rajasthan from major cities worldwide. These airlines offer various travel classes, amenities, and routes to cater to different preferences and budgets. Some popular international airlines serving Rajasthan include:

- **Emirates:** Known for its extensive global network, Emirates offers flights to Jaipur, connecting travelers from cities worldwide through its hub in Dubai.

- **British Airways:** Operating flights to major cities in India, including Jaipur, British Airways provides connectivity for travelers coming from the United Kingdom and beyond.

- **Lufthansa:** The German airline Lufthansa serves international travelers with flights to Jaipur, offering options for those flying from Europe and other continents.

- **Qatar Airways:** Qatar Airways connects Rajasthan to destinations across the Middle East, Europe, Asia, and Africa, with Doha as a major transit point.

- **Air India:** As the national carrier, Air India operates international flights to Rajasthan, connecting the state to various countries.

- **Ethiopian Airlines:** Providing connectivity to Africa, Ethiopian Airlines serves Jaipur, offering options for travelers from the African continent.

Visa and Entry Requirements: Before planning international travel to Rajasthan, it is essential to be aware of India's visa requirements and regulations. Travelers typically need a valid tourist visa, and the application process can be completed through the official website of the Indian government or the respective embassy or consulate. The visa application usually requires submitting essential documents such as a

Chapter 3

Getting Around the City

From the bustling markets of Jaipur to the serene lakes of Udaipur, here's a comprehensive guide on getting around the cities of Rajasthan.

1. Auto Rickshaws:

Jaipur: Auto rickshaws, also known as tuk-tuks, are a popular and affordable mode of transportation in Jaipur. These three-wheeled vehicles are ideal for short distances and offer a quick and convenient way to navigate through the city's narrow lanes and bustling markets. It's advisable to negotiate the fare before starting the journey, and many auto rickshaws in Jaipur operate on a metered system.

Jodhpur: Similarly, in Jodhpur, auto rickshaws are readily available for local travel. They provide a flexible and cost-effective option for exploring the city's historic sites, such as Mehrangarh Fort and the vibrant markets of the Old City.

2. Cycle Rickshaws:

Jaipur and Udaipur: For a more leisurely pace, especially in areas with narrow streets, cycle rickshaws are a charming way to experience the cities. In Jaipur and Udaipur, cycle rickshaws are commonly found around popular tourist areas, offering a unique and eco-friendly mode of transportation.

3. Taxis:

Taxis in Jaipur and Other Cities: Taxis are readily available in major cities like Jaipur, and they provide a comfortable and convenient option for getting around. In Jaipur, for example, pre-paid taxi services are available at the airport and railway station, ensuring a hassle-free experience for arriving tourists. Many taxis are equipped with meters, but it's advisable to confirm the fare before starting the journey.

4. Ride-Sharing Services:

Rajasthan Cities: Cities like Jaipur and Udaipur have embraced ride-sharing services, providing another convenient option for travelers. Popular services like Uber and Ola operate in these cities, allowing visitors to book rides through mobile applications. This modern mode of transportation offers transparency in pricing and the convenience of door-to-door service.

5. Bicycles and E-Bikes:

Jaipur: Some cities, including Jaipur, have introduced bicycle-sharing programs, allowing residents and tourists to explore the city on two wheels. These programs often include designated bike stations where users can pick up and drop off bicycles. Additionally, the emergence of e-bikes provides an eco-friendly and efficient means of transportation for short distances.

6. Public Buses:

City Bus Services: Several cities in Rajasthan operate public bus services that connect different neighborhoods and major landmarks. While these buses may be crowded, they offer an economical way to travel within the city. Information about routes and schedules can be obtained from local authorities or bus terminals.

7. Private Car Rentals:

Rental Services: For those who prefer the flexibility of private transportation, car rental services are available in major cities. Rental agencies offer a range of vehicles, including standard cars and luxury options, providing the freedom to explore the city at one's own pace. It's advisable to familiarize oneself with local traffic regulations and road conditions before opting for self-driven car rentals.

8. Rickshaws and Tongas:

Udaipur and Other Cities: In cities like Udaipur, traditional forms of transportation, such as cycle rickshaws and horse-drawn tongas, add a nostalgic touch to the local experience. These charming modes of transport are well-suited for leisurely rides around picturesque areas, allowing visitors to soak in the ambiance of the city.

9. Walking:

Exploring Old City Areas: Many of Rajasthan's cities, especially their historic cores, are best explored on foot. Walking through the narrow lanes of the Old City areas in Jaipur, Jodhpur, and Udaipur reveals hidden gems, including vibrant markets, ancient temples, and architectural marvels. Walking tours, guided or self-guided, offer an immersive experience, allowing visitors to appreciate the intricate details of the cityscape.

10. Shared Jeeps and Vans:

Rural Areas and Excursions: For travelers venturing into the outskirts or rural areas surrounding cities, shared jeeps and vans are common modes of transport. These vehicles provide connectivity to nearby villages and attractions, offering an authentic experience of rural life in Rajasthan.

11. Camel and Elephant Rides:

Tourist Attractions: In cities like Jaipur, camel and elephant rides are popular attractions, especially around iconic sites such as Amer Fort. While not practical for everyday transportation, these experiences add a touch of regality and are often enjoyed by visitors exploring the cultural heritage of Rajasthan.

Getting around the cities of Rajasthan is an integral part of the travel experience, offering a diverse range of transportation options to suit various preferences and budgets.

Public Transportation Tips in Rajasthan

Here are valuable tips for making the most of public transportation in Rajasthan.

1. **Understanding the Bus System:**

City Buses: Many cities in Rajasthan operate local bus services that connect different neighborhoods and major attractions. Jaipur, for example, has an extensive city bus network that facilitates affordable and accessible travel. Understanding the bus routes, stops, and schedules is crucial for efficient navigation.

Inter-City Buses: Inter-city buses provide connectivity between major cities and towns in Rajasthan. These buses are a cost-effective means of travel, and it's essential to check the departure points, schedules, and ticketing options in advance. Rajasthan State Road Transport Corporation (RSRTC) is a prominent operator for inter-city bus services.

2. **Using Trains for Inter-City Travel:**

Railway Connectivity: Rajasthan boasts a well-developed railway network connecting major cities and towns. Trains offer a comfortable and scenic way to travel between destinations. Booking train tickets in advance is advisable, especially during peak tourist seasons. Major railway stations in Rajasthan include Jaipur Junction, Jodhpur Junction, and Udaipur City.

Luxury Trains: For a truly regal experience, consider exploring Rajasthan on luxury trains like the Palace on Wheels, Maharajas' Express, or Royal Rajasthan on Wheels. These trains provide a blend of opulence and cultural experiences while traversing through the state's landscapes.

3. **Auto Rickshaws and Cycle Rickshaws:**

Negotiating Fares: Auto-rickshaws and cycle rickshaws are popular modes of transport for short distances within cities. It's advisable to negotiate fares in advance or ensure that meters are used to avoid any misunderstandings. Familiarize yourself with standard fare ranges to ensure a fair deal.

Tipping: Tipping is not compulsory, but it is customary to tip auto-rickshaw drivers a small amount as a gesture of appreciation for good service.

4. **Ride-Sharing Services:**

Uber and Ola: Ride-sharing services like Uber and Ola operate in cities such as Jaipur and Udaipur. These services provide a convenient and transparent way to travel, allowing users to book rides through mobile applications. Familiarize yourself with the app interface and payment methods for a seamless experience.

5. **Public Behavior and Etiquette:**

Cultural Sensitivity: Respect local customs and norms when using public transportation. Modest clothing and polite behavior are appreciated, especially in shared spaces.

Queue Discipline: Maintain discipline while waiting in queues, whether at bus stops or railway stations. This ensures a smooth boarding process and minimizes chaos.

6. **Navigating Railway Stations:**

Arrival in Advance: Arrive at railway stations well in advance, especially if you need to collect tickets or locate your platform. Stations can be busy, and having extra time allows for unforeseen delays.

Porter Services: If you have heavy luggage, consider utilizing porter services available at railway stations. Porters can assist with carrying luggage and navigating through crowded areas.

7. **Ticketing and Reservations:**

Advance Booking: For trains and buses, consider booking tickets in advance, especially during peak seasons. This ensures availability and allows you to plan your itinerary more effectively.

Online Platforms: Use online platforms for ticket reservations and bookings. Websites and mobile apps for railway and bus services provide convenience and real-time information.

8. **Understanding Peak Hours:**

Rush Hours: Be aware of peak commuting hours, especially in larger cities. Plan your travel accordingly to avoid the crowds and potential delays.

Whether you're exploring the Pink City of Jaipur or the Blue City of Jodhpur, embracing the diversity of public transportation adds a layer of authenticity to your adventure in this culturally rich state.

Traveling to Rajasthan Nearby Cities

Traveling to nearby cities from Rajasthan opens up a realm of exploration, allowing visitors to witness diverse landscapes, cultural nuances, and historical treasures.

Agra, Uttar Pradesh:

Distance from Jaipur: Agra, home to the iconic Taj Mahal, is approximately 240 kilometers (149 miles) from Jaipur. The journey takes around 4 to 5 hours by road, making it a feasible day trip or an overnight excursion.

Historical Marvels: Agra, steeped in Mughal history, boasts architectural marvels that transcend time. The Taj Mahal, a UNESCO World Heritage Site and one of the New Seven Wonders of the World, stands as an eternal symbol of love. A visit to the Agra Fort and Fatehpur Sikri provides further insight into the Mughal era's grandeur.

Travel Tips:

- Plan an early morning visit to the Taj Mahal to witness the sunrise, offering a magical ambiance.
- Consider exploring Agra's vibrant markets for handicrafts and traditional artifacts.
- Engage in a guided tour to uncover the historical significance of each monument.

2. **Delhi:**

Distance from Jaipur: Delhi, the capital city of India, is approximately 270 kilometers (168 miles) from Jaipur. The journey can take around 5 to 6 hours by road, depending on traffic conditions.

Cultural and Historical Extravaganza: Delhi, with its contrasting Old and New parts, is a treasure trove of history, culture, and modernity. Explore the historic Red Fort, Qutub Minar, India Gate, and Humayun's Tomb. Dive into the bustling lanes of Old Delhi to experience the vibrant chaos of Chandni Chowk and visit the serene Lotus Temple.

Travel Tips:

- Allocate sufficient time to explore both Old and New Delhi, each offering a distinct flavor.
- Try the street food in Chandni Chowk for an authentic taste of Delhi's culinary delights.
- Utilize the Delhi Metro for efficient and quick transportation between attractions.

3. **Pushkar, Rajasthan:**

Distance from Jaipur: Pushkar, known for its sacred lake and vibrant spirituality, is approximately 145 kilometers

(90 miles) from Jaipur. The journey takes around 2 to 3 hours by road.

Spiritual Retreat: Pushkar is a significant pilgrimage site with the Brahma Temple and the holy Pushkar Lake at its heart. The town is renowned for its annual Pushkar Camel Fair, attracting travelers and traders from around the world. The tranquil ambiance and spiritual aura make Pushkar a serene escape from the bustling city life.

Travel Tips:

- Attend the Pushkar Camel Fair if your visit coincides with the annual event, typically held in November.
- Explore the local markets for handicrafts, textiles, and traditional Rajasthani artifacts.
- Partake in the spiritual rituals at Pushkar Lake for a tranquil experience.

4. Udaipur, Rajasthan:

Distance from Jaipur: Udaipur, often referred to as the City of Lakes, is approximately 394 kilometers (245 miles) from Jaipur. The journey by road can take around 6 to 7 hours.

City of Lakes and Palaces: Udaipur, surrounded by picturesque lakes and adorned with palaces, is a romantic destination. Visit the majestic City Palace, explore the Jag Mandir and Jag Niwas islands on Lake Pichola, and wander through the vibrant markets of the old city. Udaipur's charm lies in its scenic beauty and regal architecture.

Travel Tips:

- Take a boat ride on Lake Pichola for panoramic views of the City Palace and surrounding landscapes.
- Visit the Jagdish Temple and the Saheliyon Ki Bari to witness Udaipur's cultural and architectural heritage.
- Explore the local markets for traditional Rajasthani handicrafts and textiles.

5. **Jaisalmer, Rajasthan:**

Distance from Jodhpur: Jaisalmer, known as the Golden City, is approximately 285 kilometers (177 miles) from Jodhpur. The road journey takes around 5 to 6 hours.

Desert Beauty and Fortresses: Jaisalmer, nestled in the Thar Desert, is famous for its golden sand dunes and the formidable Jaisalmer Fort. Explore the intricately carved havelis, take a camel safari in the desert, and witness the mesmerizing sunset over the dunes. Jaisalmer offers a unique blend of history, culture, and the magic of the desert.

Travel Tips:

- Experience a night stay in a desert camp for an authentic taste of Rajasthan's desert life.
- Wander through the narrow lanes of the Jaisalmer Fort and visit the Patwon Ki Haveli.
- Attend cultural performances, such as folk dances and music, in the evening for an immersive experience.

6. Bikaner, Rajasthan:

Distance from Jaipur: Bikaner, renowned for its medieval architecture and the Karni Mata Temple, is approximately 330 kilometers (205 miles) from Jaipur. The journey by road takes around 6 to 7 hours.

Historical Splendor: Bikaner is home to the majestic Junagarh Fort, known for its impressive architecture and rich history. Explore the Lalgarh Palace, visit the Karni Mata Temple (known for its rat population), and stroll through the vibrant bazaars showcasing traditional crafts and textiles.

Travel Tips:

- Taste the famous Bikaneri snacks, such as bhujia and rasgulla, for a culinary treat.
- Visit the National Research Centre on Camel for insights into the importance of camels in the region.
- Explore the Rampuria Havelis for a glimpse into Bikaner's architectural heritage.

7. **Ajmer, Rajasthan:**

Distance from Jaipur: Ajmer, known for the Ajmer Sharif Dargah, is approximately 135 kilometers (84 miles) from Jaipur. The journey by road takes around 2 to 3 hours.

Spiritual and Historical Hub: Ajmer is a significant pilgrimage site with the revered Ajmer Sharif Dargah attracting devotees from various faiths. The city also houses the serene Ana Sagar Lake, the Adhai Din Ka Jhonpra, and the Akbari Fort. Ajmer's spiritual ambiance and historical landmarks make it a compelling destination.

Travel Tips:

- Visit the Dargah Sharif during the Urs festival for a cultural and spiritual experience.
- Explore the Taragarh Fort for panoramic views of Ajmer and its surroundings.

- Enjoy a boat ride on Ana Sagar Lake for a peaceful retreat.

8. **Mount Abu, Rajasthan:**

Distance from Udaipur: Mount Abu, the only hill station in Rajasthan, is approximately 163 kilometers (101 miles) from Udaipur. The road journey takes around 3 to 4 hours.

Hill Station Retreat: Nestled in the Aravalli Range, Mount Abu offers a refreshing escape with its cool climate and lush landscapes. Visit the Dilwara Temples, explore Nakki Lake, and enjoy panoramic views from the Sunset Point. The tranquil environment and architectural marvels make Mount Abu a unique destination in Rajasthan.

Travel Tips:

- Explore the Nakki Lake area for shopping, boating, and enjoying local cuisine.
- Visit the Achalgarh Fort and Guru Shikhar for breathtaking views of the surrounding hills.
- Attend the Summer Festival held in May for cultural performances and festivities.

9. **Jodhpur, Rajasthan:**

Distance from Jaisalmer: Jodhpur, the Blue City, is approximately 285 kilometers (177 miles) from Jaisalmer. The road journey takes around 5 to 6 hours.

Majestic Forts and Blue Hues: Jodhpur is renowned for the Mehrangarh Fort, a colossal fortress perched on a rocky hill. Explore the Umaid Bhawan Palace, wander through the vibrant markets of the old city, and savor the view of the blue-painted houses from the fort. Jodhpur's architectural marvels and cultural richness make it a captivating destination.

Travel Tips:

- Take a guided tour of Mehrangarh Fort to delve into its history and architectural significance.
- Explore the bustling Sardar Market for handicrafts, textiles, and local spices.
- Visit the Jaswant Thada, a serene marble cenotaph, for a peaceful retreat.

10. **Chittorgarh, Rajasthan:**

Distance from Udaipur: Chittorgarh, known for its formidable fort, is approximately 115 kilometers (71 miles) from Udaipur. The journey by road takes around 2 to 3 hours.

Historical Fort and Temples: Chittorgarh Fort, a UNESCO World Heritage Site, stands as a testament to Rajput valor and resilience. Explore the massive fort complex, visit the Vijay Stambh and Kirti Stambh, and witness the serene beauty of Rana Kumbha's Palace. Chittorgarh's historical significance and architectural wonders make it a compelling destination.

Travel Tips:

- Engage in the light and sound show at Chittorgarh Fort for a captivating historical narrative.
- Visit the Meera Temple and Kalika Mata Temple within the fort complex for spiritual experiences.
- Explore the nearby Bassi Wildlife Sanctuary for nature enthusiasts.

11. **Kota, Rajasthan:**

Distance from Jaipur: Kota, known for its engineering and coaching institutes, is approximately 250 kilometers (155 miles) from Jaipur. The road journey takes around 5 to 6 hours.

Educational Hub and Forts: Kota is a city that blends educational excellence with historical richness. Visit the Kota Barrage, explore the City Palace and Jag Mandir, and take a boat ride on the Chambal River. Kota's unique combination of academic vibrancy and cultural heritage makes it an interesting destination.

Travel Tips:

- Explore the Seven Wonders Park showcasing replicas of the world's iconic monuments.

- Visit the Garh Palace for its architectural grandeur and panoramic views of the city.
- Take a boat safari in the Chambal River for a unique wildlife experience.

12. **Alwar, Rajasthan:**

Distance from Jaipur: Alwar, known for its historical forts and wildlife sanctuaries, is approximately 150 kilometers (93 miles) from Jaipur. The road journey takes around 3 to 4 hours.

Historical Heritage and Sariska Tiger Reserve: Alwar is home to the majestic Alwar Fort, the haunted Bhangarh Fort, and the Sariska Tiger Reserve. Explore the architectural wonders, witness the vibrant markets, and embark on a wildlife safari in Sariska. Alwar's blend of history and natural beauty makes it an intriguing destination.

Travel Tips:

- Visit the Siliserh Lake Palace for a serene retreat by the lakeside.
- Explore the Bala Quila for panoramic views of the city and surrounding landscapes.
- Engage in wildlife photography during a safari in the Sariska Tiger Reserve.

13. **Bharatpur, Rajasthan:**

Distance from Jaipur: Bharatpur, renowned for its bird sanctuary, is approximately 180 kilometers (112 miles) from Jaipur. The road journey takes around 3 to 4 hours.

Keoladeo National Park: Bharatpur is home to the Keoladeo National Park, a UNESCO World Heritage Site and a haven for birdwatchers. Explore the diverse avian species, take a boat ride through the marshes, and witness the migratory birds during the winter season. Bharatpur's natural beauty and wildlife make it an ideal destination for nature enthusiasts.

Travel Tips:

- Hire a local guide for birdwatching to enhance your experience in Keoladeo National Park.
- Visit the Lohagarh Fort and the Bharatpur Palace for insights into the region's history.
- Plan your visit during the winter months for the best birdwatching opportunities.

14. **Neemrana, Rajasthan:**

Distance from Jaipur: Neemrana, known for its historical fort and palace, is approximately 128 kilometers (80 miles) from Jaipur. The road journey takes around 2 to 3 hours.

Historical Fort and Zip Lining: Neemrana Fort, a 15th-century heritage hotel, offers a glimpse into Rajasthan's regal past. Explore the fort's architecture, enjoy a zip-lining adventure, and savor the panoramic views from the ramparts. Neemrana's combination of history, adventure, and hospitality makes it a unique destination.

Travel Tips:

- Stay overnight at the Neemrana Fort Palace for a royal experience and sunset views.
- Participate in the thrilling zip-lining activities offered within the fort complex.
- Explore the nearby Baori for a stepwell experience showcasing architectural ingenuity.

15. **Sikar, Rajasthan:**

Distance from Jaipur: Sikar, known for its havelis and frescoed mansions, is approximately 114 kilometers (71 miles) from Jaipur. The road journey takes around 2 to 3 hours.

Architectural Heritage: Sikar is renowned for its rich architectural heritage, with havelis like the Laxmangarh Fort and the Madho Niwas Kothi showcasing exquisite frescoes. Explore the vibrant markets, witness the grandeur of the forts, and delve into the region's artistic legacy. Sikar's cultural and historical treasures make it a hidden gem.

Travel Tips:

- Take a heritage walk through the old town to appreciate the frescoes adorning the mansions.
- Visit the Harshnath Temple and the Jeen Mata Temple for spiritual experiences.
- Engage with local artisans to witness the traditional crafts and artwork of Sikar.

16. **Ranthambore, Rajasthan:**

Distance from Jaipur: Ranthambore, renowned for its tiger reserve, is approximately 160 kilometers (99 miles) from Jaipur. The road journey takes around 3 to 4 hours.

Tiger Safaris and Forts: Ranthambore National Park is a wildlife enthusiast's paradise, offering opportunities to spot tigers, leopards, and a variety of wildlife species. Explore the Ranthambore Fort, visit the Padam Talao lake, and embark on thrilling safaris for a unique blend of nature and history. Ranthambore's biodiversity and historical landmarks make it an exciting destination.

Travel Tips:

- Book safari permits in advance, especially during peak tourist seasons, for assured entry.

- Visit the Trinetra Ganesh Temple within the Ranthambore Fort for a spiritual experience.
- Engage in birdwatching around the park's numerous water bodies.

17. **Sawai Madhopur, Rajasthan:**

Distance from Jaipur: Sawai Madhopur, the gateway to Ranthambore National Park, is approximately 130 kilometers (81 miles) from Jaipur. The road journey takes around 2 to 3 hours.

Wildlife Hub and Temples: Apart from being the entry point to Ranthambore, Sawai Madhopur has its own cultural and historical attractions. Visit the Ranthambore School of Art, explore the Chamatkar Temple, and experience the local lifestyle. Sawai Madhopur's unique combination of wildlife and heritage makes it an intriguing stopover.

Travel Tips:

- Interact with local artisans at the Ranthambore School of Art to appreciate their craftsmanship.
- Explore the nearby Kala Gaura Bhairav Temple and the Shilpgram for cultural insights.
- Attend the annual Ranthambore Festival for a celebration of wildlife and culture.

18. Shekhawati, Rajasthan:

Distance from Jaipur: Shekhawati, known for its painted havelis, is approximately 168 kilometers (104 miles) from Jaipur. The road journey takes around 3 to 4 hours.

Open-Air Art Gallery: Shekhawati is a treasure trove of artistic heritage, with its towns and villages adorned with intricately painted havelis and mansions. Explore the towns of Mandawa, Nawalgarh, and Fatehpur for a mesmerizing experience of open-air art. Shekhawati's painted havelis and frescoed walls make it a unique cultural destination.

Travel Tips:

- Take a guided tour to fully appreciate the stories and details depicted in the frescoes.
- Explore the Dundlod Fort and the Hanuman Prasad Goenka Haveli for architectural marvels.
- Visit during the Shekhawati Festival for a celebration of art, music, and cultural heritage.

19. Pilani, Rajasthan:

Distance from Jaipur: Pilani, known for its educational institutions, is approximately 217 kilometers (135 miles) from Jaipur. The road journey takes around 4 to 5 hours.

Educational Excellence and Birla Temples: Pilani is synonymous with the Birla Institute of Technology and Science (BITS Pilani), a prestigious educational institution. Explore the BITS Pilani campus, visit the Birla Museum, and witness the Birla Temples dedicated to various deities. Pilani's blend of education and spirituality makes it a unique destination.

Travel Tips:

- Check for any special events or festivals happening within the BITS Pilani campus.
- Visit the Saraswati Temple and the Ganesha Temple for a spiritual retreat.
- Interact with students and faculty members to gain insights into the academic culture.

20. Banswara, Rajasthan:

Distance from Udaipur: Banswara, known for its natural beauty and tribal culture, is approximately 160 kilometers (99 miles) from Udaipur. The road journey takes around 3 to 4 hours.

Scenic Landscapes and Tribal Heritage: Banswara, nestled amidst the Aravalli Hills, offers a serene retreat with its lakes, forests, and tribal communities. Visit the Anand Sagar Lake, explore the Mahi Dam, and experience the tribal traditions of the Bhil community.

Banswara's tranquility and cultural richness make it a hidden gem in southern Rajasthan.

Travel Tips:

- Take a boat ride on the Anand Sagar Lake for a peaceful experience surrounded by nature.
- Engage in local cultural activities and traditions with the Bhil tribes.
- Explore the Tripura Sundari Temple and the Madareshwar Temple for spiritual insights.

Venturing to nearby cities from Rajasthan opens up a kaleidoscope of experiences, from exploring historical marvels and spiritual retreats to embracing diverse landscapes and vibrant cultures.

Chapter 4

Travel essentials in Rajasthan

Here's a brief list of travel essentials for your Rajasthan adventure.

1. **Travel Documents:**

   - **Passport and Visa:** Ensure your passport is valid for at least six months beyond your planned departure date. Obtain the appropriate visa for your stay in India.

   - **Travel Insurance:** Consider purchasing travel insurance that covers medical emergencies, trip cancellations, and other unforeseen events.

   - **Flight and Hotel Confirmations:** Keep printed or digital copies of your flight tickets, hotel reservations, and any other important booking confirmations.

   - **Identification:** Carry a government-issued photo ID, such as a driver's license, as a form of identification.

2. **Health and Safety:**

- **Prescription Medications:** Pack any prescription medications you may need, along with a copy of your prescription.

- **First Aid Kit:** Include basic first aid supplies like bandages, pain relievers, antiseptic wipes, and any personal medications.

- **Travel Health Essentials:** Consider vaccinations or medications for diseases prevalent in the region, and carry insect repellent, sunscreen, and hand sanitizer.

- **Emergency Contact Information:** Keep a list of emergency contacts, including local emergency numbers and contact information for your embassy or consulate.

3. **Clothing and Footwear:**

- **Light and Comfortable Clothing:** Rajasthan can be hot, especially during summer. Pack lightweight and breathable fabrics like cotton. Long sleeves and pants can provide protection from the sun.

- **Comfortable Footwear:** Bring comfortable walking shoes, especially if you plan to explore historical sites and markets. Sandals or open-toed shoes are suitable for warmer weather.

- **Modest Attire:** Be mindful of local customs and dress modestly, especially when visiting religious sites. Consider packing a shawl or scarf for covering shoulders.

4. **Travel Gear:**

   - **Backpack or Daypack:** Carry a small backpack for day trips, sightseeing, and carrying essentials.

   - **Power Adapter:** Rajasthan uses the Type C and Type D electrical outlets. Bring a suitable power adapter for your devices.

   - **Reusable Water Bottle:** Stay hydrated by carrying a reusable water bottle. Consider a bottle with a built-in filter for areas where water quality might be a concern.

   - **Travel Pillow and Blanket:** For comfort during long journeys or flights, consider a travel pillow and a lightweight blanket.

5. **Technology and Communication:**

   - **Mobile Phone:** Ensure your phone is unlocked for international use and get a local SIM card for affordable communication.

- **Camera:** Capture the stunning landscapes and cultural experiences with a camera or smartphone.

- **Portable Charger:** Keep your devices charged on the go with a portable charger or power bank.

- **Language Translation App:** Download a language translation app to assist with communication, especially if you're not fluent in Hindi.

6. **Money and Finances:**

- **Currency:** Carry Indian Rupees (INR) in small denominations for local transactions. Larger cities also accept credit/debit cards.

- **ATM and Credit Cards:** ATMs are widely available, but it's advisable to carry some cash. Inform your bank of your travel plans to avoid card issues.

- **Money Belt:** Use a money belt or neck pouch to keep your valuables, such as money, passport, and cards, secure.

7. **Travel Guides and Maps:**

- **Guidebook:** Bring a travel guidebook or download travel apps to learn about local attractions, customs, and useful tips.

- **Map of Rajasthan:** Carry a physical map or use online maps for navigation in unfamiliar areas.

8. **Sun Protection and Hygiene:**

   - **Sun Hat and Sunglasses:** Protect yourself from the intense sun with a wide-brimmed hat and sunglasses.

   - **Sunscreen:** Use a high SPF sunscreen to shield your skin from the strong sunlight.

   - **Wet Wipes and Hand Sanitizer:** Keep wet wipes and hand sanitizer for maintaining hygiene, especially when water may not be readily available.

9. **Cultural Considerations:**

   - **Respectful Attire:** Dress modestly, especially when visiting religious sites or rural areas.

   - **Cultural Sensitivity:** Familiarize yourself with local customs and practices to show respect to the local culture.

10. **Miscellaneous:**

    - **Travel Locks:** Use travel locks to secure your luggage, especially during train or bus journeys.

    - **Umbrella or Rain Jacket:** While Rajasthan is mostly arid, unexpected rain can occur. Carry a compact umbrella or rain jacket.

- **Snacks:** Bring non-perishable snacks for times when local cuisine may not be readily available.

- **Entertainment:** Pack a book, e-reader, or other forms of entertainment for downtime during travel.

11. Local Information:

- **Local SIM Card:** Purchase a local SIM card for your phone to have access to local networks and data services.

- **Emergency Numbers:** Save local emergency numbers, including police, medical, and your country's embassy or consulate.

- **Public Transportation Information:** If using public transport, keep schedules and information handy for reference.

12. Shopping Bag:

- **Reusable Shopping Bag:** Carry a foldable or reusable shopping bag for any purchases you make during your travels.

Things to know before you travel to Rajasthan

1. **Cultural Diversity:** Rajasthan is known for its rich cultural heritage, and each city within the state has its own unique traditions and customs. Be prepared to encounter diverse festivals, art forms, and languages as you travel from one city to another.

2. **Traditional Attire:** Embrace the local culture by trying on traditional Rajasthani attire. Women often wear colorful ghagras (skirts) and odhnis (veils), while men don turbans and dhotis. You may find it interesting to participate in the vibrant local fashion.

3. **Religious Sensitivity:** Rajasthan has numerous religious sites, and it's essential to be respectful when visiting temples, mosques, and other places of worship. Dress modestly and follow any specific guidelines provided at each religious site.

4. **Local Markets and Bargaining:** The bustling markets of Rajasthan, such as Jaipur's Johari Bazaar and Jodhpur's Sardar Market, are a shopper's paradise. Bargaining is a common practice in these markets, so be prepared to negotiate prices when shopping for traditional handicrafts, textiles, and jewelry.

5. **Festival Calendar:** Rajasthan hosts various festivals throughout the year. Check the festival calendar before planning your trip to see if you can experience

vibrant celebrations like Diwali, Holi, or the Pushkar Camel Fair, depending on your travel dates.

6. **Cash Availability:** While larger cities have ATMs and card payment options, it's advisable to carry some cash, especially when visiting rural areas or local markets where electronic transactions may not be as prevalent.

7. **Time Zone:** Rajasthan operates on Indian Standard Time (IST), which is UTC+5:30. Adjust your schedule accordingly and be aware of any time zone differences if you plan to coordinate with people in other regions.

8. **Trekking and Adventure Activities:** If you're interested in trekking or adventure activities, Rajasthan offers opportunities in areas like Mount Abu and the Aravalli Range. Check the local guidelines and hire experienced guides for a safe and enjoyable experience.

9. **Wildlife Sanctuaries:** Rajasthan is home to several wildlife sanctuaries, including Ranthambore National Park. If you plan to visit these areas, check for the best safari seasons and adhere to wildlife conservation guidelines.

By keeping these aspects in mind, you can make the most of your journey through Rajasthan, appreciating its cultural richness, historical significance, and warm hospitality.

Local customs and etiquette in Rajasthan

Here are some key aspects of local customs and etiquette in Rajasthan:

1. **Attire and Dress Code:**
   - Rajasthanis often dress modestly, especially in rural areas and religious sites. It's advisable for visitors to follow suit, covering shoulders and knees when entering temples or participating in cultural events.

2. **Respect for Elders:**
   - Elders are highly respected in Rajasthan. When interacting with older individuals, it is customary to use respectful titles such as "ji" (similar to "Mr." or "Mrs.") after their names.

3. **Removal of Footwear:**
   - When entering someone's home, religious sites, or certain shops, it is customary to remove footwear. Pay attention to cues from locals and observe whether others are removing their shoes.

4. **Dining Etiquette:**
   - When dining in a traditional setting, it's common for people to sit cross-legged on the floor. Wash your hands before and after meals. Accepting food or tea when offered is a sign of hospitality.

5. **Gift Giving:**
   - If invited to someone's home, bringing a small gift is considered a polite gesture. It could be sweets, flowers, or a small token of appreciation.

6. **Public Affection:**
   - Public displays of affection are generally frowned upon in traditional settings. It's advisable to maintain a level of modesty in public spaces.

7. **Photography Etiquette:**
   - Always seek permission before taking photographs of individuals, especially in rural areas. Some people may have cultural or religious reasons for not wanting to be photographed.

8. **Temple Etiquette:**
   - When visiting temples, cover your head with a scarf or a hat, remove your shoes, and avoid taking photographs inside unless permitted. Dress modestly to show respect for the sacred space.

9. **Respect for Sacred Objects:**
   - Treat religious and sacred objects with respect. Avoid touching religious artifacts or sacred texts in temples unless given permission.

10. **Ceremonial Practices:**
    - Rajasthan has various rituals and ceremonies associated with weddings, festivals, and religious events. If you're invited to participate, observe and follow the lead of locals to show respect.

11. **Haggling in Markets:**
    - Bargaining is a common practice in local markets. However, do it with a smile and maintain a friendly attitude. It's part of the cultural experience and can be enjoyable for both parties.

12. **Pilgrimages and Religious Sites:**
    - When visiting pilgrimage sites or religious festivals, be mindful of the devout atmosphere. Keep noise levels low and avoid disruptive behavior.

13. **Interaction with Locals:**
    - Rajasthanis are known for their hospitality. Engage with locals respectfully, ask questions about their culture, and show genuine interest in their way of life.

14. **Participation in Traditional Activities:**
    - If invited to participate in traditional activities such as folk dances, music, or ceremonies, embrace the opportunity. It's a chance to not only learn about

the culture but also to bond with the local community.

15. **Respect for Caste and Community Traditions:**
    - Rajasthan has diverse communities and castes, each with its own traditions. Be aware of and respect the specific customs and practices of different communities.

16. **Conservative Dress in Rural Areas:**
    - In rural areas, the dress code tends to be more conservative. It's advisable to dress modestly and follow the local norms to avoid any unintentional cultural misunderstandings.

17. **Tipping Practices:**
    - Tipping is common in restaurants, hotels, and for services like guided tours or transportation. While there may not be a fixed percentage, offering a gratuity for good service is appreciated.

By being attentive to these customs and etiquette, visitors can enjoy a more immersive and respectful experience in Rajasthan.

Safety and emergency information of Rajasthan

Here are key points to consider for a safe and secure visit to Rajasthan:

1. **Health Precautions:**

   o Stay hydrated, especially during the hot summer months. Drink bottled or purified water.

   o Use sunscreen to protect against the strong sun, and carry insect repellent, especially if visiting rural or wildlife areas.

   o Be cautious about street food and ensure that any food consumed is from reputable establishments.

2. **Medical Facilities:**

   o Larger cities in Rajasthan, such as Jaipur and Udaipur, have well-equipped hospitals and medical facilities. However, in rural areas, medical resources may be limited. Have a basic first aid kit and any necessary medications.

3. **Travel Insurance:**

   o It's highly advisable to have comprehensive travel insurance that covers medical emergencies, trip cancellations, and evacuation if needed.

4. **Local Laws and Customs:**
   - Familiarize yourself with local laws and customs to avoid any unintentional legal issues. For example, drug offenses can lead to severe penalties.

5. **Emergency Numbers:**
   - Save important local emergency numbers, including police (100), ambulance (102), and fire (101), in your phone. Know the location of the nearest police station and hospital.

6. **Local SIM Card:**
   - Get a local SIM card for your phone to ensure easy communication. This is particularly important in case of emergencies.

7. **Accommodation Safety:**
   - Choose reputable and well-reviewed accommodations. Ensure that your hotel or guesthouse has secure locks and follows safety standards.

8. **Transportation Safety:**
   - Use authorized and reliable transportation services. When using taxis or rickshaws, agree on the fare before starting the journey.

9. **Valuables and Personal Belongings:**
    - Keep your valuables, such as passports, money, and electronics, secure. Use hotel safes when available, and avoid displaying expensive items in public.

10. **Weather Awareness:**
    - Be aware of weather conditions, especially during the monsoon season (July to September). Heavy rainfall can lead to flooding in some areas.

11. **Wildlife Safety:**
    - If visiting wildlife reserves or sanctuaries, follow safety guidelines provided by authorities. Maintain a safe distance from animals, and do not feed or provoke them.

12. **Cultural Sensitivity:**
    - Respect local customs and traditions to avoid unintentional misunderstandings. Dress modestly, especially when visiting religious sites.

13. **Traffic and Road Safety:**
    - Exercise caution when crossing roads, and use designated crosswalks. Be aware of traffic rules and drive defensively if renting a vehicle.

14. **Emergency Exit Plan:**
    - Familiarize yourself with emergency exits in your accommodation and any public places you visit.

15. **Severe Weather Precautions:**
    - In the event of severe weather conditions such as dust storms, follow local advisories and take shelter indoors.

16. **Political and Social Situations:**
    - Stay informed about local news and be aware of any political or social situations that may affect your travel plans. Avoid participating in or getting close to any political demonstrations or unrest.

17. **Local Assistance:**
    - If you encounter any issues or emergencies, seek assistance from local authorities, your country's embassy or consulate, or your hotel.

By staying informed, being prepared, and exercising caution, you can have a safe and enjoyable experience in Rajasthan.

Chapter 5

Where To Stay in Rajasthan

Accommodation options in Rajasthan

1. Heritage Hotels: Rajasthan is renowned for its grand palaces and forts, many of which have been transformed into luxurious heritage hotels. These opulent properties provide an opportunity to experience the regal lifestyle of the bygone era. The City Palace in Udaipur, Rambagh Palace in Jaipur, and Umaid Bhawan Palace in Jodhpur are exemplary instances of heritage hotels that seamlessly blend history with modern comforts.

2. Boutique Havelis: For a more intimate and personalized experience, consider staying in boutique havelis. These are typically smaller, privately-owned properties, often old mansions or courtyard residences, converted into charming guesthouses. The intricate architecture, traditional décor, and warm hospitality make boutique havelis a unique accommodation choice. The Haveli Dharampura in Delhi and Jasvilas in Jaipur are prime examples.

3. Luxury Resorts: Rajasthan's diverse topography includes picturesque deserts, lush forests, and serene lakes, providing a canvas for luxurious resorts. These resorts offer an oasis of comfort and relaxation. The

Oberoi Udaivilas in Udaipur, Suryagarh in Jaisalmer, and Amanbagh in Alwar exemplify the epitome of luxury, providing not just accommodation but a holistic experience.

4. Budget Hotels: Travelers on a budget can find a plethora of affordable options in Rajasthan. Budget hotels, guesthouses, and hostels are available in popular tourist destinations, providing comfortable stays without burning a hole in the pocket. These accommodations are often located in proximity to major attractions and offer basic amenities for a convenient stay.

5. Camps and Tents: For a unique experience in the desert regions, consider staying in camps and tents. Jaisalmer and Pushkar, in particular, offer desert camping experiences where you can sleep under the stars in the heart of the Thar Desert. These accommodations provide a blend of rustic charm and modern comfort.

6. Eco-friendly Retreats: With a growing emphasis on sustainable tourism, Rajasthan has witnessed the emergence of eco-friendly retreats. These accommodations focus on minimizing their environmental impact while providing guests with a peaceful and nature-centric experience. The Tree of Life Resort & Spa in Jaipur and Chhatra Sagar in Pali are notable examples.

7. Mid-range Hotels: Mid-range hotels in Rajasthan offer a balance between comfort and affordability. These hotels provide well-appointed rooms, essential amenities, and often feature on-site restaurants serving local and international cuisine. They are ideal for travelers seeking a comfortable stay without the extravagance of luxury accommodations.

8. Guesthouses and Homestays: For a more immersive cultural experience, consider staying in guesthouses or homestays. This option allows you to interact closely with locals, experience their way of life, and gain insights into the regional culture. Homestays in places like Jaipur, Udaipur, and Jodhpur offer a home-like atmosphere and personalized hospitality.

9. Chain Hotels: International and domestic hotel chains have a significant presence in major cities of Rajasthan. These hotels offer standardized services, modern amenities, and the familiarity of a recognized brand. They cater to business travelers and tourists looking for a reliable and consistent stay experience.

10. Houseboats in Udaipur: Udaipur's tranquil lakes provide an opportunity to stay in charming houseboats. Floating on the serene waters of Lake Pichola, these houseboats offer a unique accommodation experience with panoramic views of the surrounding landscapes and the city's palaces.

Hotels And Resorts

Luxury Accommodations in Rajasthan

1. **The Oberoi Udaivilas, Udaipur:**
    - **Address:** Haridasji Ki Magri, Mulla Talai, Udaipur, Rajasthan 313001, India.
    - **Offerings:** Set on the shores of Lake Pichola, The Oberoi Udaivilas is a luxurious retreat that exudes opulence. The hotel features intricately designed rooms and suites with lake views, private pools, and personalized butler service. The property boasts multiple dining options, a spa, and stunning gardens. Guests can enjoy boat rides on the lake and cultural performances.
    - **Price Range:** USD 800 - USD 2,000 per night.

2. **Rambagh Palace, Jaipur:**
    - **Address:** Bhawani Singh Road, Rambagh, Jaipur, Rajasthan 302005, India.
    - **Offerings:** Once the residence of the Maharaja of Jaipur, Rambagh Palace is a Taj hotel that epitomizes regal living. The palace offers luxurious rooms, suites, and historical suites adorned with royal

artifacts. Guests can indulge in fine dining at multiple restaurants, rejuvenate at the Jiva Grande Spa, and experience the royal heritage during a stay at this grand property.

- **Price Range:** USD 600 - USD 1,800 per night.

3. **Suryagarh, Jaisalmer:**

    - **Address:** Kahala Phata, Sam Road, Jaisalmer, Rajasthan 345001, India.
    - **Offerings:** Located in the heart of the Thar Desert, Suryagarh is a fortress-style luxury hotel that combines heritage and modern comforts. The hotel offers tastefully decorated rooms and suites, a spa, an outdoor pool, and a range of dining options serving local and international cuisine. Guests can partake in desert safaris, cultural performances, and stargazing experiences.
    - **Price Range:** USD 400 - USD 1,200 per night.

4. **Umaid Bhawan Palace, Jodhpur:**

    - **Address:** Circuit House Rd, Cantt Area, Jodhpur, Rajasthan 342006, India.

- **Offerings:** Umaid Bhawan Palace, managed by Taj Hotels, is an imposing structure set amidst 26 acres of lush gardens. The palace offers lavish accommodations with views of the city or the palace gardens. Guests can dine at the fine-dining restaurants, enjoy a vintage car ride, and relax at the Jiva Spa. The palace also houses a museum showcasing its royal history.
- **Price Range:** USD 600 - USD 2,000 per night.

5. **The Serai, Jaisalmer:**

    - **Address:** Bherwa, Jaisalmer - Sam - Dhanana Rd, Jaisalmer, Rajasthan 345001, India.
    - **Offerings:** Nestled in the dunes of the Thar Desert, The Serai offers luxury tented accommodations with modern amenities. The tents are spacious and well-appointed, providing a unique blend of comfort and desert living. The property features a spa, an outdoor pool, and dining experiences under the starlit sky. Guests can engage in desert safaris and cultural activities.
    - **Price Range:** USD 400 - USD 1,000 per night.

Mid-Range Options in Rajasthan

1. **The Fern An Ecotel Hotel, Jaipur:**
   - **Address:** Plot No. 3, Airport Plaza, Tonk Road, Chandrakala Colony, Mata colony, Jaipur, Rajasthan 302018, India.
   - **Offerings:** The Fern is an environmentally conscious hotel offering modern amenities at an affordable price. The rooms are well-equipped, and the hotel features a rooftop pool, fitness center, and multiple dining options. Its eco-friendly practices make it an ideal choice for conscious travelers.
   - **Price Range:** USD 70 - USD 150 per night.

2. **Zone By The Park, Jodhpur:**
   - **Address:** 5, 5th, Chopasni, Jodhpur, Rajasthan 342001, India.
   - **Offerings:** Zone by The Park is a contemporary hotel that provides comfortable rooms, a rooftop pool, and vibrant interiors. The hotel offers a fitness center, a lounge bar, and a multi-cuisine restaurant. Its central location makes it convenient for exploring Jodhpur's attractions.
   - **Price Range:** USD 60 - USD 120 per night.

3. **Mandawa Kothi, Mandawa:**
   - **Address:** V&A Farm, Mandawa, Rajasthan 333704, India.
   - **Offerings:** Mandawa Kothi is a heritage-style hotel that captures the essence of Rajasthan's architecture. The hotel offers elegantly decorated rooms, a courtyard, and a swimming pool. Guests can enjoy traditional Rajasthani cuisine at the in-house restaurant and explore the nearby Mandawa Fort and Havelis.
   - **Price Range:** USD 50 - USD 100 per night.

4. **Hotel Lake Palace, Udaipur:**
   - **Address:** 62, Gangaur Ghat, Above Jagdish Temple, Udaipur, Rajasthan 313001, India.
   - **Offerings:** Overlooking Lake Pichola, Hotel Lake Palace is a mid-range option with comfortable rooms and a rooftop terrace offering panoramic views. The hotel provides a restaurant serving Indian and international cuisine. Its proximity to major attractions like Jagdish Temple and City Palace adds to its appeal.
   - **Price Range:** USD 60 - USD 130 per night.

5. **Hotel Tokyo Palace, Pushkar:**

    o **Address:** Choti Basti, Pushkar, Rajasthan 305022, India.

    o **Offerings:** Situated near Pushkar Lake, Hotel Tokyo Palace offers budget-friendly yet comfortable accommodations. The hotel features a garden, a terrace, and a rooftop restaurant with views of the city and the lake. Guests can explore the nearby Brahma Temple and enjoy the vibrant atmosphere of Pushkar.

    o **Price Range:** USD 40 - USD 80 per night.

Budget-Friendly Stays in Rajasthan

1. **Zostel Jaipur:**

    o **Address:** 85-A, Panchsheel Enclave, JLN Marg, near Hotel Clarks Amer, Jaipur, Rajasthan 302018, India.

    o **Offerings:** Zostel Jaipur is a budget-friendly hostel offering dormitory-style accommodations and private rooms. The hostel provides a communal kitchen, a common area for socializing, and organized activities for guests. Its vibrant atmosphere makes it a popular choice for budget travelers.

    o **Price Range:** USD 10 - USD 30 per night.

2. **Moustache Hostel, Jodhpur:**

   - **Address:** S-49, Sardarpura, Umaid Club Road, Jodhpur, Rajasthan 342001, India.

   - **Offerings:** Moustache Hostel in Jodhpur caters to budget travelers seeking a sociable atmosphere. The hostel offers dormitory beds, private rooms, and communal spaces for socializing. With a rooftop terrace providing panoramic views of the city, it's an ideal choice for those looking for affordability without compromising on experience.

   - **Price Range:** USD 10 - USD 25 per night.

3. **Hotel Shekhawati, Mandawa:**

   - **Address:** Near Poddar Chowk, Ward No. 6, Mandawa, Rajasthan 333704, India.

   - **Offerings:** Hotel Shekhawati is a budget-friendly option in the heart of Mandawa. The hotel provides simple yet comfortable rooms, a restaurant serving local cuisine, and a convenient location for exploring Mandawa's heritage sites and vibrant streets.

   - **Price Range:** USD 20 - USD 50 per night.

4. **Garden View Hotel, Udaipur:**

- **Address:** 1/2 Gangaur Ghat Marg, Near Jagdish Chowk, Udaipur, Rajasthan 313001, India.
- **Offerings:** Garden View Hotel offers budget accommodations in the scenic city of Udaipur. The hotel features basic yet clean rooms, a garden, and a rooftop restaurant with views of Lake Pichola. Its central location makes it accessible to major attractions like Jagdish Temple and the City Palace.
- **Price Range:** USD 25 - USD 60 per night.

5. **Mystic Jaisalmer Hotel & Restaurant:**

   - **Address:** K.L Anchalvansi Colony, On Fort Kotari Para, Dhibba Para, Jaisalmer, Rajasthan 345001, India.
   - **Offerings:** Mystic Jaisalmer is a budget-friendly hotel located near Jaisalmer Fort. The hotel offers simple rooms, a restaurant serving local and international dishes, and a rooftop terrace with panoramic views of the fort and the city. Its affordability and proximity to attractions make it suitable for budget-conscious travelers.
   - **Price Range:** USD 15 - USD 40 per night.

Alternative Lodging

Bed and Breakfasts in Rajasthan

1. **Jaipur Friendly Villa:**

   - **Address:** 4, Gokul Vihar, Jagatpura Road, Malviya Nagar, Jaipur, Rajasthan 302017, India.

   - **Offerings:** Jaipur Friendly Villa is a charming bed and breakfast that offers comfortable rooms with traditional decor. The property features a garden, a shared lounge, and a terrace. Guests can enjoy a complimentary breakfast and personalized service from the friendly hosts. The location provides easy access to Jaipur's major attractions.

   - **Price Range:** INR 2,000 - INR 4,000 per night.

2. **Mandore Guest House, Jodhpur:**

   - **Address:** Mandore Road, Paota, Jodhpur, Rajasthan 342006, India.

   - **Offerings:** Nestled in the historic city of Jodhpur, Mandore Guest House is a cozy B&B surrounded by lush gardens. The guesthouse offers well-appointed rooms, a courtyard, and a restaurant serving local cuisine. Guests can experience the tranquility of Mandore Gardens nearby and explore the cultural heritage of the region.

- Price Range: INR 1,500 - INR 3,500 per night.

3. **Ganpati Guest House, Pushkar:**
   - **Address:** Near Pushkar Lake, Chotti Basti, Pushkar, Rajasthan 305022, India.
   - **Offerings:** Ganpati Guest House is a family-run B&B located near the holy Pushkar Lake. The guesthouse provides simple yet comfortable rooms, a rooftop terrace with panoramic views, and a vegetarian restaurant. Guests can immerse themselves in the spiritual ambiance of Pushkar and participate in the vibrant local culture.
   - **Price Range:** INR 1,000 - INR 2,500 per night.

4. **Bundi Vilas, Bundi:**
   - **Address:** 2, Nawal Sagar, Lake, Near Purani Kotwali, Bundi, Rajasthan 323001, India.
   - **Offerings:** Situated on the banks of Nawal Sagar Lake, Bundi Vilas is a bed and breakfast offering picturesque views and personalized service. The property features elegantly decorated rooms, a rooftop terrace, and a garden. Guests can enjoy the historical charm of Bundi and explore nearby attractions such as Taragarh Fort.
   - **Price Range:** INR 1,500 - INR 3,000 per night.

5. **Udai Haveli Guest House, Udaipur:**
   - **Address:** 1, Harshvardhan Marg, Outside Chandpole, Udaipur, Rajasthan 313001, India.
   - **Offerings:** Udai Haveli Guest House is a traditional B&B located in the heart of Udaipur. The guesthouse offers comfortable rooms, a courtyard, and a rooftop terrace with views of the City Palace. Guests can experience the hospitality of Udaipur and explore the nearby attractions, including Jagdish Temple.
   - **Price Range:** INR 1,500 - INR 3,500 per night.

Vacation Rentals in Rajasthan

1. **Heritage Haveli, Jaipur (Airbnb):**
   - **Address:** Civil Lines, Jaipur, Rajasthan 302006, India.
   - **Offerings:** Heritage Haveli is a vacation rental available on Airbnb, offering a unique stay in a heritage property. The rental includes spacious rooms, traditional decor, and access to the haveli's amenities. Guests can enjoy a private and authentic experience while exploring the vibrant city of Jaipur.
   - **Price Range:** INR 3,000 - INR 7,000 per night.

2. **Desert Rose House, Jaisalmer (Vrbo):**
   - **Address:** K.L Anchalvansi Colony, On Fort Kotari Para, Dhibba Para, Jaisalmer, Rajasthan 345001, India.
   - **Offerings:** Desert Rose House is a vacation rental listed on Vrbo, providing a comfortable stay near Jaisalmer Fort. The rental includes well-appointed rooms, a kitchenette, and a terrace with fort views. Guests can enjoy a homely atmosphere and explore the historical wonders of Jaisalmer.
   - **Price Range:** INR 2,500 - INR 5,000 per night.

3. **Aravalli View Villa, Mount Abu (Booking.com):**
   - **Address:** Near Sant Sarovar, Mount Abu, Rajasthan 307501, India.
   - **Offerings:** Aravalli View Villa is a vacation rental available on Booking.com, offering a tranquil retreat in Mount Abu. The villa features spacious rooms, a garden, and a terrace with panoramic views of the Aravalli Range. Guests can experience the serene ambiance of Mount Abu and visit nearby attractions.
   - **Price Range:** INR 2,000 - INR 4,500 per night.

4. **Riverside Cottage, Rishikesh (MakeMyTrip):**

- **Address:** Shivpuri, Rishikesh, Rajasthan 249201, India.
- **Offerings:** Riverside Cottage is a vacation rental listed on MakeMyTrip, providing a scenic getaway in Rishikesh. The cottage offers cozy accommodations, river views, and proximity to adventure activities. Guests can enjoy the tranquility of the Ganges and explore the spiritual and adventurous side of Rishikesh.
- **Price Range:** INR 2,500 - INR 6,000 per night.

5. **Pushkar Lakeview Homestay, Pushkar (Expedia):**
   - **Address:** Near Varah Ghat, Choti Basti, Pushkar, Rajasthan 305022, India.
   - **Offerings:** Pushkar Lakeview Homestay is a vacation rental available on Expedia, offering a homely atmosphere near Pushkar Lake. The homestay provides comfortable rooms, a garden, and a terrace with lake views. Guests can experience the tranquility of Pushkar and participate in the town's vibrant cultural events.
   - **Price Range:** INR 1,500 - INR 3,500 per night.

These bed and breakfasts and vacation rentals in Rajasthan offer a diverse range of experiences, from heritage charm to scenic retreats. Whether opting for a cozy B&B with personalized service or a vacation rental for a private stay, these accommodations provide an authentic and memorable way to explore the cultural richness of Rajasthan.

Things to consider when deciding where to stay in Rajasthan

Here are essential factors to consider when deciding where to stay in Rajasthan:

1. Location:

- Consider the location of your accommodation in relation to the attractions you plan to visit. In cities like Jaipur and Udaipur, staying in the historical city center puts you in proximity to major landmarks, markets, and cultural sites. For a tranquil experience, opt for accommodations near lakes or on the outskirts of cities.

2. Type of Experience:

- Define the type of experience you seek. If you desire a regal experience, choose a heritage hotel or palace-turned-hotel in cities like Jaipur, Jodhpur, or Udaipur. For a more immersive cultural experience, consider staying in a traditional haveli or a guesthouse in the heart of the old city.

3. Budget:

- Establish a budget range for your accommodation. Rajasthan offers a wide spectrum of options, from luxury hotels and resorts to budget-friendly guesthouses and hostels. Knowing your budget beforehand allows you to narrow down your choices and find the best value for your money.

4. Amenities and Facilities:

- Consider the amenities and facilities offered by the accommodation. Luxury hotels may provide spa services, fine dining restaurants, and pools, while budget options focus on essentials. Ensure the chosen accommodation aligns with your preferences for comfort, services, and recreational facilities.

5. Season and Weather:

- Rajasthan experiences diverse weather conditions, from scorching summers to cool winters. Consider the time of year you plan to visit and choose accommodation accordingly. In summer, look for properties with pools, and in winter, those with cozy fireplaces and heating facilities.

6. Cultural Immersion:

- If you seek a deeper connection with local culture, opt for accommodations that promote cultural immersion. This could include heritage homestays, where you live with a local family, or boutique hotels showcasing traditional architecture and decor.

7. Transportation Accessibility:

- Check the accessibility of transportation from your accommodation. For convenient exploration, choose a place with easy access to public transportation, or consider accommodations that offer shuttle services. Proximity to railway stations and airports can also be a deciding factor.

8. Reviews and Ratings:

- Read reviews and ratings from fellow travelers on platforms like TripAdvisor, Booking.com, or Google reviews. Feedback from others who have stayed at the property can provide insights into the overall experience, service quality, and any potential issues.

9. Safety and Security:

- Prioritize safety and security when selecting accommodation. Choose well-established hotels or reputable guesthouses with positive reviews. Check if the property has secure entrances, well-lit areas, and, if necessary, additional security measures.

10. Special Requirements:

- If you have specific requirements, such as accessibility features, pet-friendly accommodations, or family-friendly facilities, communicate these needs with the accommodation provider before booking. Clarifying special requirements ensures a comfortable stay.

11. Local Events and Festivals:

- Check if there are any local events or festivals during your stay. Choosing accommodation close to the venue or within the festivities can add to the vibrancy of your experience. However, if you prefer a quieter stay, consider accommodations away from the event areas.

12. Unique Offerings:

- Some accommodations offer unique experiences, such as rooftop views of city landmarks, cooking classes, or guided tours. Explore these offerings to enhance your stay and make it more memorable.

13. Duration of Stay:

- The duration of your stay can influence the type of accommodation you choose. For a short visit, you might prioritize staying in the heart of the city to maximize exploration. For longer stays, consider options that offer more extensive amenities and a relaxed environment.

14. Booking Platforms:

- Utilize various booking platforms to explore a range of accommodations. Compare prices, read reviews, and check for exclusive deals or promotions on different platforms to find the best value for your chosen stay.

Considering these factors when deciding where to stay in Rajasthan ensures that your accommodation aligns with your preferences, enhances your travel experience, and provides a comfortable and enjoyable base for exploring the captivating landscapes and cultural richness of this enchanting state.

Chapter 6

Practical Tips

Budget

Here's a breakdown of potential expenses for a trip to Rajasthan:

1. Flights:

- Round-trip international flights to India can vary significantly based on your departure location, the time of booking, and the airline. Estimate anywhere from $700 to $1500 or more for a return ticket.

2. Accommodation:

- Accommodation costs vary based on your choice of hotels, guesthouses, or resorts. Rajasthan offers a wide range of options, from budget stays to luxury hotels. On average, budget and mid-range options might cost between $30 to $100 per night, while luxury accommodations can range from $150 to $500 or more per night.

3. Transportation:

- Within Rajasthan, transportation costs will depend on your mode of travel. Domestic flights, trains, and buses are common options. A rough estimate for transportation within the state could be around $50 to $100 per day, depending on distances covered and the mode of transport.

4. Food:

- Food costs can vary based on your dining preferences. Street food and local eateries are more budget-friendly, while fine dining establishments may be more expensive. On average, budgeting around $20 to $40 per day for meals is a reasonable estimate.

5. Sightseeing and Activities:

- Entrance fees to attractions, guided tours, and activities can add up. Budgeting around $10 to $30 per day for sightseeing is a general estimate.

6. Miscellaneous Expenses:

- This category includes expenses such as SIM cards, tips, souvenirs, and miscellaneous items. A budget of around $10 to $20 per day should cover these additional costs.

7. Travel Insurance:

- It's highly recommended to have travel insurance, and the cost will depend on factors like coverage, duration, and your age. A rough estimate might be $5 to $15 per day.

8. Contingency:

- It's wise to have some funds set aside for unexpected expenses or additional activities you might decide to do during your trip. A contingency budget of around 10% of your total estimated expenses is a good rule of thumb.

Total Estimated Budget:

- Considering the above estimates, a daily budget for a mid-range traveler might range from $125 to $300 or more. For a week-long trip, this could translate to a total budget of $875 to $2,100, excluding international flights.

Remember that these are general estimates, and actual costs can vary. It's advisable to research specific costs based on your preferences, book accommodations and transportation in advance when possible, and factor in any additional activities or special experiences you plan to include in your itinerary.

Language and communication of Rajasthan

Rajasthan, with its rich cultural tapestry, boasts a diverse linguistic landscape that reflects the state's historical and geographical influences. The primary languages spoken in Rajasthan are Hindi and Rajasthani, each with its unique dialects and variations. Additionally, due to the state's popularity as a tourist destination, English is widely understood in urban areas and tourist hubs.

1. Hindi:

- Hindi serves as the official language of the state and is spoken by a majority of the population. It acts as a unifying force, allowing people from different regions and linguistic backgrounds to communicate effectively. In cities and towns, Hindi is commonly used in official documents, educational institutions, and day-to-day interactions.

2. Rajasthani:

- Rajasthani is a group of Indo-Aryan languages spoken by the people of Rajasthan. It has several dialects, including Marwari, Mewari, Dhundhari, and Harauti, each prevalent in specific regions. Marwari, spoken in the Marwar region, is one of the most widely spoken dialects and is often used in business, local markets, and social interactions. Mewari is predominant in the Udaipur region, and Dhundhari is spoken in the Jaipur area.

3. English:

- English is increasingly becoming a lingua franca, especially in urban centers and areas frequented by tourists. In major cities like Jaipur, Udaipur, and Jodhpur, where tourism plays a significant role, English is commonly spoken and understood in hotels, restaurants, and tourist attractions. This linguistic adaptability caters to the diverse international audience that visits Rajasthan.

4. Tribal Languages:

- Rajasthan is home to various tribal communities, each with its distinct languages. Languages such as Bhili, Garasia, and Meena are spoken by specific tribal groups. These languages contribute to the state's linguistic diversity, reflecting the cultural richness of Rajasthan's indigenous communities.

5. Sign Language and Gestures:

- In rural and remote areas, where linguistic diversity is more pronounced, non-verbal communication through gestures and expressions becomes crucial. Locals often use traditional gestures and signs to convey messages, facilitating communication even when there is a language barrier.

Cultural Influence on Communication:

- Rajasthan's culture significantly influences the way people communicate. Politeness and respect are paramount in interactions, and traditional greetings like "Namaste" are commonly used. The use of titles, such as "ji" or "saheb," adds a touch of respect to conversations. Social niceties and courtesies play an integral role in day-to-day communication.

Challenges and Opportunities:

- While Hindi and Rajasthani serve as the primary means of communication, the linguistic diversity in the state can pose challenges for effective communication, especially in rural areas. However, this diversity also presents an opportunity for visitors to immerse themselves in the local culture by learning a few basic phrases in the regional dialects.

Preservation of Heritage Languages:

- Efforts are being made to preserve and promote Rajasthan's linguistic heritage. Cultural events, folk performances, and literary festivals often celebrate the diversity of languages in the state, contributing to the preservation of linguistic traditions.

Embracing the linguistic richness of Rajasthan enhances the overall experience, fostering a deeper connection with the people and the heritage of this enchanting state.

Arts and Theaters in Rajasthan

Rajasthan is a treasure trove of traditional arts and vibrant theatrical performances. The state's artistic expressions are deeply rooted in its history, reflecting the royal patronage and the diverse influences of different dynasties. From folk arts to royal court traditions, Rajasthan offers a kaleidoscopic view of artistic endeavors that captivate the senses and tell tales of its cultural legacy.

1. **Folk Arts:**

- Rajasthan is renowned for its colorful and expressive folk arts, each representing the unique traditions of various regions. One of the most famous forms is **Rajasthani Folk Dance**, which includes captivating performances like Ghoomar, Kalbeliya, and Bhavai. These dances, accompanied by lively music and vibrant costumes, showcase the joyous spirit of the state's rural communities.

Puppetry:

- Puppetry is an ancient art form that has thrived in Rajasthan. **Rajasthani Puppetry,** also known as Kathputli, involves intricately crafted wooden puppets that come to life in the hands of skilled puppeteers. These performances narrate folk tales, legends, and historical events, providing entertainment while preserving cultural narratives.

Art and Craft:

- Rajasthan is a hub of exquisite arts and crafts, with skilled artisans creating intricate works that reflect the state's royal aesthetics. **Miniature Paintings** from places like Jaipur and Nathdwara are known for their detailed depictions of myths, legends, and courtly life. **Blue Pottery** from Jaipur, **Bandhani** textiles from Jodhpur and tie-and-dye fabrics from Ajmer showcase the diverse artistic expressions found in everyday objects.

Theaters and Cultural Performances:

- The vibrant cultural landscape of Rajasthan extends to theaters and cultural performances. Cities like Jaipur and Udaipur have thriving cultural centers and theaters that host a variety of performances, including plays, musicals, and dance dramas. These venues provide a platform for contemporary artists to showcase their talents while preserving traditional art forms.

Festivals and Melas:

- Rajasthan's festivals and melas are grand showcases of its artistic prowess. The **Pushkar Camel Fair**, for example, goes beyond being a livestock fair to become a cultural extravaganza with traditional performances, music, and camel decoration contests. Similarly, the **Jaipur Literature Festival** brings together literary enthusiasts and serves as a platform for discussions on literature, arts, and culture.

Royal Patronage:

- The royal courts of Rajasthan were historically patrons of the arts, fostering an environment where artists could flourish. Palaces like the **City Palace in Jaipur** and the **Udaipur City Palace** showcase not only architectural splendor but also house museums that display royal artifacts and artistic creations, offering a glimpse into the opulent artistic heritage.

Contemporary Art Scene:

- Rajasthan's art scene is not confined to traditional forms alone. The state has seen a burgeoning contemporary art movement with galleries and art festivals showcasing the works of modern artists. **Jawahar Kala Kendra** in Jaipur is a significant cultural institution that promotes contemporary visual arts and performances.

Chapter 7
Cultural Experiences

Best Traditional Foods to Try in Rajasthan

From savory delights to sweet treats, here are some of the best traditional foods to try in Rajasthan:

1. Dal Baati Churma:

- A quintessential Rajasthani dish, Dal Baati Churma is a hearty and flavorful combination. Baatis are wheat flour balls baked or grilled, served with dal (lentils) and churma (sweet crushed wheat mixed with ghee and sugar). This dish is a wholesome and filling delight that showcases the essence of Rajasthani cuisine.

2. Laal Maas:

- For those who enjoy spicy and robust flavors, Laal Maas is a must-try. This fiery red curry is made with succulent mutton, a blend of spices, and a generous amount of red chili. Laal Maas is a dish that originated from the royal kitchens of

Rajasthan and is a testament to the love for spice in the region.

3. Gatte ki Sabzi:

- Gatte ki Sabzi is a popular vegetarian dish that features gram flour dumplings (gatte) cooked in a yogurt-based curry. The dumplings are seasoned with various spices, giving the dish a distinctive taste. Gatte ki Sabzi is often served with steamed rice or Indian bread.

4. Ker Sangri:

- Ker Sangri is a traditional Rajasthani dish made from dried berries (ker) and beans (sangri) found in the arid regions of the state. These sun-dried ingredients are cooked with various spices to create a unique and tangy dish. Ker Sangri is often enjoyed with Indian bread like roti or bajra ki roti.

5. Mohan Maas:

- Mohan Maas is a delicacy fit for royalty. This slow-cooked mutton dish is prepared in a rich and flavorful gravy made with milk, cream, and a blend of aromatic spices. Mohan Maas showcases the royal culinary skills of Rajasthan and is a dish reserved for special occasions.

6. Rajasthani Kadi:

- Rajasthani Kadi is a variation of the popular North Indian dish, but with a distinct Rajasthani touch. This yogurt-based curry is thickened with gram flour and flavored with a medley of spices. It is often served with steamed rice or khichdi, offering a comforting and flavorful meal.

7. Bajra Roti with Lasun Chutney:

- Bajra (pearl millet) is a staple crop in Rajasthan, and Bajra Roti is a traditional bread made from this nutritious grain. It is often paired with Lasun Chutney, a garlic-based condiment that adds a burst of flavor. The combination of Bajra Roti and Lasun Chutney is a simple yet delightful culinary experience.

8. Mawa Kachori:

- Indulge your sweet tooth with Mawa Kachori, a delectable dessert that originated in the city of Jodhpur. These deep-fried pastries are filled with a mixture of khoya (reduced milk), nuts, and aromatic spices. Mawa Kachori is often dipped in sugar syrup, making it a rich and irresistible treat.

9. Pyaaz Kachori:

- Pyaaz Kachori is a popular street food in Rajasthan that features deep-fried pastries filled with a spiced onion mixture. The crispy exterior and flavorful stuffing make it a favorite snack, often enjoyed with tamarind chutney or yogurt.

10. Rabri:

- Rabri is a luscious dessert made by reducing and thickening milk over low heat. It is sweetened with sugar and flavored with cardamom and saffron, creating a rich and indulgent treat. Rabri is often garnished with chopped nuts and served chilled.

Best restaurants in Rajasthan

1. Spice Court, Jaipur:

- **Address:** Achrol House, Jacob Road, Civil Lines, Jaipur, Rajasthan 302006, India.

- **Specialty:** Spice Court is renowned for its diverse menu offering authentic Rajasthani cuisine, including specialties like Dal Baati Churma, Laal Maas, and Gatte ki Sabzi. The restaurant also serves a variety of Indian and international dishes.

- **Price Range:** USD 15 - USD 30 per person.

2. Suvarna Mahal, Jaipur:

- **Address:** Rambagh Palace, Bhawani Singh Road, Jaipur, Rajasthan 302005, India.

- **Specialty:** Located in the opulent Rambagh Palace, Suvarna Mahal is a fine-dining restaurant serving royal Rajasthani and Indian delicacies. The regal ambiance complements the exquisite dishes, making it a dining experience fit for royalty.

- **Price Range:** USD 40 - USD 100 per person.

3. Chokhi Dhani, Jaipur:

- **Address:** 12 Miles Tonk Road, Via Vatika, Jaipur, Rajasthan 303905, India.

- **Specialty:** Chokhi Dhani is not just a restaurant but an immersive cultural experience. Known for its Rajasthani village theme, guests can enjoy traditional Rajasthani cuisine in a setting that replicates a rural village environment. The extensive thali offers a variety of dishes.
- **Price Range:** USD 20 - USD 40 per person.

4. **Peshawri, Jodhpur:**

- **Address:** Umaid Bhawan Palace, Circuit House Road, Jodhpur, Rajasthan 342006, India.
- **Specialty:** Situated in the majestic Umaid Bhawan Palace, Peshawri is renowned for its North-West Frontier cuisine. The restaurant specializes in kebabs, tandoori dishes, and Indian bread, offering a delightful gastronomic journey in a regal setting.
- **Price Range:** USD 30 - USD 80 per person.

5. **Indique, Udaipur:**

- **Address:** 40, Lal Ghat, Behind Jagdish Temple, Udaipur, Rajasthan 313001, India.
- **Specialty:** Overlooking the serene Lake Pichola, Indique offers a picturesque dining experience along with a menu featuring a fusion of Indian,

Rajasthani, and Continental cuisines. The rooftop setting provides a romantic ambiance, perfect for a special evening.

- **Price Range:** USD 25 - USD 50 per person.

6. Jagat Niwas Palace Hotel Rooftop Restaurant, Udaipur:

- **Address:** 23-25 Lal Ghat, Udaipur, Rajasthan 313001, India.

- **Specialty:** Perched on the rooftop of Jagat Niwas Palace Hotel, this restaurant offers panoramic views of Lake Pichola and the City Palace. The menu includes a mix of Indian, Rajasthani, and international dishes, providing a delightful culinary experience in a historical setting.

- **Price Range:** USD 20 - USD 40 per person.

7. 1135 AD, Amer:

- **Address:** Amer Road, Jal Mahal, Jaipur, Rajasthan 302002, India.

- **Specialty:** Housed in the historic Amer Fort, 1135 AD offers a unique dining experience amidst regal surroundings. The menu features a blend of Rajasthani, Indian, and Mughlai cuisines. The restaurant's name pays homage to the year when Amer was founded.

- **Price Range:** USD 30 - USD 70 per person.

8. The Oberoi Udaivilas, Udaipur:

- **Address:** Haridasji Ki Magri, Mulla Talai, Udaipur, Rajasthan 313001, India.

- **Specialty:** The Oberoi Udaivilas offers a luxurious dining experience at its various restaurants, including Udaimahal and Suryamahal. These restaurants serve an array of international and Indian cuisines in a regal setting overlooking Lake Pichola.

- **Price Range:** USD 50 - USD 150 per person.

9. Samode Haveli, Jaipur:

- **Address:** Gangapole, Jaipur, Rajasthan 302002, India.

- **Specialty:** The restaurant at Samode Haveli offers a charming dining experience within a historic haveli. The menu features a selection of Rajasthani and North Indian dishes prepared with a focus on traditional flavors. The serene courtyard adds to the ambiance.

- **Price Range:** USD 25 - USD 60 per person.

10. Rawat Mishtan Bhandar, Jaipur:

- **Address:** Station Road, Sindhi Camp, Jaipur, Rajasthan 302001, India.

- **Specialty:** Rawat Mishtan Bhandar is a renowned sweets shop and restaurant in Jaipur, famous for its Pyaaz Kachori and other Rajasthani sweets and snacks. It offers a casual dining experience, perfect for trying local snacks and desserts.

- **Price Range:** USD 5 - USD 15 per person.

These restaurants in Rajasthan offer not only exquisite cuisine but also a diverse range of dining experiences, from royal elegance to cultural immersion.

Top shopping areas in Rajasthan

Here are some of the top shopping areas in the Rajasthan:

1. **Johari Bazaar, Jaipur:**

    - **Location:** Johari Bazaar, Jaipur, Rajasthan.
    - **Highlights:** Known as the 'Jeweler's Market,' Johari Bazaar is a bustling marketplace in the heart of Jaipur. It is famous for its exquisite collection of traditional Rajasthani jewelry, including Kundan, Meenakari, and precious gemstones. The market also offers textiles, handicrafts, and vibrant mojaris (traditional Rajasthani footwear).

2. **Bapu Bazaar, Jaipur:**

    - **Location:** Bapu Bazaar, Jaipur, Rajasthan.
    - **Highlights:** Bapu Bazaar is a popular market in Jaipur, known for its diverse range of products. Here, you can find everything from textiles and handicrafts to perfumes and traditional jootis (shoes). The market is particularly famous for its tie-and-dye fabrics, known as Bandhani, and Jaipuri quilts.

3. **Clock Tower Market, Jodhpur:**

- **Location:** Sardar Market, Jodhpur, Rajasthan.
- **Highlights:** The Clock Tower Market, located near the majestic Mehrangarh Fort, is a vibrant market offering a variety of handicrafts, textiles, and spices. It's an excellent place to shop for traditional Jodhpuri suits, leather goods, and antiques. The bustling atmosphere adds to the charm of the shopping experience.

4. **Sardar Market, Jaisalmer:**

   - **Location:** Sardar Market, Jaisalmer, Rajasthan.
   - **Highlights:** Situated near the Jaisalmer Fort, Sardar Market is known for its unique items like camel leather products, embroidered textiles, and Rajasthani handicrafts. The market comes alive with vibrant colors, and the shops offer a glimpse into the artistic traditions of the region.

5. **Tripolia Bazaar, Jaipur:**

   - **Location:** Tripolia Bazaar, Jaipur, Rajasthan.
   - **Highlights:** Tripolia Bazaar is renowned for its traditional lac jewelry, textiles, and ironware. The market's narrow lanes are lined with shops selling an array of products, including the famous Jaipuri quilts, vibrant textiles, and traditional Rajasthani puppets.

6. **M.I. Road, Jaipur:**

    - **Location:** M.I. Road, Jaipur, Rajasthan.

    - **Highlights:** Mirza Ismail Road, or M.I. Road, is a bustling commercial street in Jaipur. It offers a mix of traditional and modern shopping experiences. You can find shops selling jewelry, textiles, handicrafts, and boutiques showcasing contemporary fashion. The street is also dotted with cafes and eateries.

7. **Nehru Bazaar, Jaipur:**

    - **Location:** Nehru Bazaar, Jaipur, Rajasthan.

    - **Highlights:** Nehru Bazaar is famous for its collection of textiles, especially Jaipuri quilts and fabrics. The market is also known for its blue pottery, traditional footwear, and vibrant Rajasthani puppets. It's a great place to explore the local craftsmanship and pick up souvenirs.

8. **Chetak Circle, Udaipur:**

    - **Location:** Chetak Circle, Udaipur, Rajasthan.

    - **Highlights:** Chetak Circle is a shopping area in Udaipur known for its boutique stores and shops selling traditional Rajasthani clothing, jewelry, and handicrafts. The area has a relaxed ambiance, and the stores offer a mix of modern and traditional items.

9. **Clock Tower Market, Jaipur:**

   - **Location:** Clock Tower Market, Jaipur, Rajasthan.

   - **Highlights:** This market, situated near the Hawa Mahal, is known for its vibrant collection of textiles, including bandhani sarees and fabrics. You can also find traditional footwear, handicrafts, and souvenirs. The market is a visual delight with its colorful displays.

10. **Bada Bazaar, Bikaner:**

    - **Location:** Bada Bazaar, Bikaner, Rajasthan.

    - **Highlights:** Bada Bazaar in Bikaner is famous for its sweets, particularly the famous Bikaneri bhujia. The market also offers a variety of traditional Rajasthani crafts, textiles, and camel leather products. It's an excellent place to experience the local flavors and shop for unique items.

In conclusion, Rajasthan's top shopping areas provide a delightful blend of traditional and contemporary shopping experiences.

Chapter 8
Family Activities

Couples In Rajasthan

Here are some romantic things for couples to do in the royal state of Rajasthan:

1. Hot Air Balloon Ride in Jaipur:

- Soar above the Pink City and its iconic landmarks like the Hawa Mahal and Amber Fort in a hot air balloon. The breathtaking panoramic views, especially during sunrise or sunset, create a romantic and memorable experience. Companies like Sky Waltz offer hot air balloon rides for couples seeking a unique adventure.

2. Moonlit Dinner at Lake Pichola, Udaipur:

- Experience the romance of Udaipur by enjoying a moonlit dinner on a boat in Lake Pichola. The calm waters, the glimmering lights of the City Palace and Jag Mandir, and a private dinner set the stage for a magical evening. Many tour operators and hotels offer personalized boat rides and dining experiences.

3. Overnight Camping in the Thar Desert:

- Escape to the golden sands of the Thar Desert for a romantic overnight camping experience. Enjoy a private dinner under the stars, traditional music, and the tranquility of the desert surroundings. Camps like the Serai or Samsara provide luxurious glamping options for a romantic retreat.

4. Stargazing in Jaisalmer:

- The clear desert skies of Jaisalmer create a perfect setting for stargazing. Couples can embark on a stargazing tour where local experts guide them through the constellations and share fascinating stories about the night sky. This celestial experience adds a touch of wonder to a romantic evening.

5. Heritage Walks in Bundi:

- Explore the lesser-explored town of Bundi hand in hand with your partner. The town is known for its ornate step wells, intricate havelis, and historical architecture. Take a leisurely heritage walk through the narrow lanes, discovering the artistic marvels and enjoying the quiet charm of this offbeat destination.

6. Sunset Camel Safari in Pushkar:

- Venture into the serene landscapes around Pushkar on a sunset camel safari. As the sun dips below the horizon, the changing colors of the desert create a mesmerizing backdrop. Share this intimate experience with your partner while riding atop these gentle creatures, exploring the rustic beauty of the region.

7. Dinner on the Ramparts of Mehrangarh Fort, Jodhpur:

- Elevate your dining experience by having a private dinner on the ramparts of Mehrangarh Fort in Jodhpur. Many luxury hotels and tour operators arrange exclusive dinners with stunning views of the city lights below, offering couples a romantic and regal ambiance.

8. Couple's Spa Retreat in a Palace:

- Pamper yourselves with a couple's spa retreat in one of Rajasthan's heritage palaces. Many luxury hotels, such as the Umaid Bhawan Palace in Jodhpur or the Rambagh Palace in Jaipur, offer rejuvenating spa experiences set in opulent surroundings, allowing couples to unwind in regal style.

9. Culinary Workshop in Jaipur:

- Embark on a culinary journey together by participating in a traditional Rajasthani cooking class in Jaipur. Learn to prepare iconic dishes like Dal Baati Churma or Gatte ki Sabzi under the guidance of expert chefs. This hands-on experience adds a flavorful and interactive element to your romantic getaway.

10. Vintage Car Ride in Jaipur:

- Step back in time and take a vintage car ride through the streets of Jaipur. Enjoy the regal charm as you explore the city in style, seated in a classic car from the bygone era. This unique experience offers a blend of luxury and nostalgia, perfect for a romantic escapade.

Rajasthan With kids

Here are some of the best things for kids to do in Rajasthan:

1. Elephant Ride at Amer Fort, Jaipur:

- Make a visit to Amer Fort in Jaipur an unforgettable experience for kids by taking an elephant ride to the fort's entrance. The gentle giants, adorned with colorful decorations, create a magical and unique way for children to ascend the historic fort.

2. Puppet Shows in Jaipur:

- Rajasthan is famous for its traditional puppetry, and witnessing a puppet show in Jaipur is a delightful experience for kids. These vibrant and engaging performances showcase Rajasthani folklore and tales, keeping children entertained while introducing them to the state's cultural heritage.

3. Zip Lining at Mehrangarh Fort, Jodhpur:

- For adventurous kids, a thrilling zip-lining experience at Mehrangarh Fort in Jodhpur is a must-try. Soaring over the majestic fort and enjoying panoramic views of the Blue City below create an exhilarating and memorable adventure.

4. Desert Safari in Jaisalmer:

- Take kids on a unique desert safari experience in the golden sands of Jaisalmer. Whether it's a camel safari or a jeep ride, exploring the vast Thar Desert offers children an opportunity to witness the desert's beauty, spot wildlife, and enjoy the tranquility of the dunes.

5. Sound and Light Show at Chittorgarh Fort:

- Explore the history of Chittorgarh Fort through a captivating sound and light show. The dramatic illumination of the fort's architecture and the narrated tales of valor and heroism make for an educational and visually stunning experience for kids.

6. Vintage Car Museum, Udaipur:

- Uncover the fascinating world of vintage cars at the Vintage Car Museum in Udaipur. Kids can marvel at the collection of classic cars, including Rolls Royces and Cadillacs, and learn about the evolution of automobiles in a regal setting.

7. Bishnoi Village Safari, Jodhpur:

- Introduce kids to the rich rural life of Rajasthan with a Bishnoi Village Safari near Jodhpur. The safari provides a unique opportunity for children to interact with locals, witness traditional crafts, and observe wildlife in their natural habitat.

8. Camel Breeding Farm, Bikaner:

- Visit the National Research Centre on Camel in Bikaner, which houses a Camel Breeding Farm. Kids can learn about the importance of camels in desert life, witness various camel breeds, and even take a camel ride, making it an informative and enjoyable experience.

9. Butterfly Park, Jaipur:

- The Jawahar Kala Kendra in Jaipur features a Butterfly Park where kids can witness a variety of colorful butterflies in a natural habitat. The park is designed to promote awareness about butterfly conservation and provides a serene and educational setting.

10. Sariska Tiger Reserve Safari:

- For wildlife enthusiasts, a safari at Sariska Tiger Reserve offers the chance to spot a variety of animals, including tigers, leopards, and deer. Kids can enjoy the thrill of a jungle safari while learning about the importance of wildlife conservation.

11. Jantar Mantar, Jaipur:

- Explore the fascinating world of astronomy and ancient science at Jantar Mantar in Jaipur. The astronomical observatory features unique instruments that were used for timekeeping and celestial observations. It's an educational and intriguing experience for curious young minds.

12. Hawa Mahal LEGO Replica, Jaipur:

- Visit the LEGO replica of Jaipur's iconic Hawa Mahal at the LEGOLAND Discovery Center in Jaipur. Kids can marvel at the intricate LEGO model of this architectural marvel and engage in hands-on LEGO building activities, combining fun and creativity.

13. Rural Stay Experience:

- Opt for a rural stay experience in one of Rajasthan's villages. This immersive encounter allows kids to participate in traditional activities like pottery making, folk dances, and rural games, providing a unique perspective on rural life in the state.

14. Dal Baati Churma Cooking Class:

- Engage kids in a hands-on cooking class to prepare the famous Rajasthani dish, Dal Baati Churma.

Many cooking schools in Jaipur offer family-friendly classes where children can learn the art of Rajasthani cuisine and enjoy the fruits of their culinary efforts.

15. Raj Mandir Cinema, Jaipur:

- Experience the grandeur of Raj Mandir Cinema, often referred to as the "Pride of Asia." This iconic cinema in Jaipur is known for its opulent interiors and unique architecture. Watching a Bollywood movie with the family here is a cinematic and cultural delight.

Chapter 9
Outdoor Activities

Hiking and Nature Trails

Rajasthan's Varied Landscape: Rajasthan, often associated with the vast Thar Desert, surprises adventure seekers with diverse landscapes, including hills, forests, and rocky terrains. Hiking and nature trails provide a unique way to explore the state's natural beauty and witness its rich biodiversity.

1. Aravalli Range Hiking: The Aravalli Range, stretching across Rajasthan, offers an array of hiking opportunities. The hills are adorned with lush vegetation, making them an ideal escape for nature enthusiasts. Trails like the one leading to the Kumbhalgarh Fort provide breathtaking views of the surrounding valleys, creating an immersive experience for hikers.

2. Mount Abu's Tranquil Trails: Mount Abu, Rajasthan's only hill station, boasts cool climate and picturesque landscapes. The trails around Mount Abu provide a serene environment for hiking. The trek to Guru Shikhar, the highest peak in the Aravalli Range, offers panoramic views of the surrounding hills and plains.

3. Sariska Tiger Reserve Trails: While primarily known for its wildlife, Sariska Tiger Reserve also features nature trails. These trails allow visitors to explore the diverse flora and fauna of the region. The experience of hiking amidst the wilderness and catching glimpses of wildlife adds an adventurous twist to the activity.

4. Keoladeo National Park Exploration: Keoladeo National Park in Bharatpur, a UNESCO World Heritage Site, is a paradise for bird watchers and nature lovers. The park features well-marked trails that lead through wetlands and dense forests. Hiking in Keoladeo provides an opportunity to observe migratory birds, including the rare Siberian Crane.

5. Ranthambore National Park Treks: Ranthambore, famous for its tiger population, also offers trekking opportunities. Guided nature walks within the park allow visitors to witness the flora and fauna, providing a unique perspective on the rugged beauty of the terrain.

Water-based Activities

Contrasting the Arid Landscape: Despite being a predominantly arid region, Rajasthan boasts water bodies that support various water-based activities. These activities offer a refreshing break from the desert landscape and add an element of excitement to outdoor adventures.

1. Boating on Lake Pichola, Udaipur: Lake Pichola, surrounded by the majestic City Palace and Jag Mandir, is a popular destination for boating. Visitors can take a boat ride on the serene waters of the lake, enjoying views of the palaces and the surrounding hills. Sunset boat rides add a romantic touch to the experience.

2. Kayaking in Chambal River: The Chambal River, flowing through parts of Rajasthan, provides an excellent setting for kayaking. The calm waters and scenic landscapes make kayaking a thrilling yet serene activity. The Chambal region is known for its rich biodiversity, and kayakers may encounter various bird species and aquatic life during their adventure.

3. Pushkar Camel Fair Hot Air Ballooning: While the Pushkar Camel Fair is a renowned cultural event, it also offers a unique water-based activity – hot air ballooning. Drifting over the Pushkar Lake and the vibrant fairground provides a bird's-eye view of the festivities and the desert landscape beyond.

4. Rafting in River Banas: Adventure seekers can indulge in river rafting in the Banas River, particularly during the monsoon season when water levels rise. The thrilling rapids and the scenic surroundings make rafting a popular activity for those seeking an adrenaline rush in the heart of Rajasthan.

5. Sambhar Salt Lake Exploration: Sambhar Salt Lake, India's largest inland saltwater lake, offers a surreal setting for water-based activities. The lake is shallow, allowing for unique experiences like salt harvesting and bird watching. Boating on the calm, reflective surface of the lake is a peaceful and unusual water adventure.

Parks and Recreation Areas

Preserving Natural Beauty: Rajasthan takes pride in preserving its natural heritage through well-maintained parks and recreation areas. These spaces not only offer a break from urban life but also serve as havens for biodiversity and outdoor activities.

1. Central Park, Jaipur: Central Park in Jaipur is a sprawling green oasis in the heart of the city. Equipped with jogging tracks, open spaces, and vibrant flower beds, the park invites locals and tourists alike to unwind. The Musical Fountain Show in the evening adds an entertaining element to the park experience.

2. Ranthambore National Park: Beyond being a prime destination for wildlife enthusiasts, Ranthambore National Park is a vast expanse of wilderness. The park features designated zones for picnics and nature walks, allowing visitors to appreciate the natural beauty of the surroundings.

3. Nehru Park, Udaipur: Nehru Park in Udaipur offers a tranquil escape by the side of Fateh Sagar Lake. The park's well-maintained lawns, jogging tracks, and recreational facilities make it a popular spot for families and individuals looking for outdoor leisure.

4. Saheliyon Ki Bari, Udaipur: Known as the Garden of the Maidens, Saheliyon Ki Bari is a historic garden with ornamental fountains, kiosks, marble elephants, and delightful lotus pools. The well-manicured lawns and serene ambiance make it a perfect spot for a leisurely stroll and relaxation.

5. Rani Sagar, Bundi: Rani Sagar in Bundi is a scenic reservoir surrounded by hills and ancient step wells. The picturesque setting makes it an ideal spot for a picnic or a peaceful retreat. Visitors can explore the historic structures and enjoy the tranquility of this lesser-known gem.

Cycling and Biking

Discovering the Land on Two Wheels: Cycling and biking open up avenues for exploring Rajasthan's landscapes at a leisurely pace. Whether it's pedaling through historic cities or biking across the desert, these activities provide an intimate and eco-friendly way to experience the region.

1. Jaipur Cycling Tour: Jaipur, with its architectural marvels and vibrant streets, offers guided cycling tours. Exploring the Pink City on a bicycle allows visitors to cover more ground than on foot while soaking in the city's colors, sounds, and historical significance.

2. Biking Through Shekhawati's Havelis: The Shekhawati region, known for its ornate havelis adorned with frescoes, is a unique biking destination. Cyclists can pedal through the narrow lanes of towns like Mandawa and Nawalgarh, discovering the artistic treasures of the region.

3. Desert Biking in Bikaner: Adventure enthusiasts can embark on desert biking expeditions in the vast landscapes around Bikaner. Riding through the desert terrain and exploring remote villages provides an offbeat and exhilarating experience for those seeking a biking adventure in the arid region.

4. Udaipur Countryside Cycling: Udaipur's picturesque countryside, with its rolling hills and serene lakes, is perfect for cycling. Guided cycling tours take participants through the rural landscapes, allowing them to witness traditional life, visit local villages, and enjoy the natural beauty.

5. Pushkar Camel Fair Bike Rally: The Pushkar Camel Fair hosts a unique bike rally that combines the thrill of biking with the cultural richness of the fair. Participants can ride through the vibrant fairground and the surrounding desert, creating a memorable biking experience amidst the festive atmosphere.

Chapter 10

Nightlife in Rajasthan

Nightlife in Rajasthan: A Cultural Extravaganza Under the Stars

Rajasthan, known for its vibrant heritage, opulent palaces, and colorful traditions, offers a unique and culturally infused nightlife that differs from the bustling city lights found in metropolitan areas. While not synonymous with the energetic nightlife scenes of some urban centers, Rajasthan's evenings are characterized by cultural performances, traditional music, and the mystical ambiance of its historic surroundings.

Hawa Mahal Night View, Jaipur: The iconic Hawa Mahal in Jaipur takes on a different allure at night. Illuminated with warm lights, the "Palace of Winds" becomes a captivating sight. While there might not be bustling nightclubs, the architectural marvels of Rajasthan become illuminated masterpieces, and visitors often take leisurely strolls around these structures, appreciating their grandeur against the night sky.

Lakeside Serenity in Udaipur: Udaipur, known as the "City of Lakes," offers a serene and picturesque nightlife around its pristine lakes. Visitors can enjoy boat rides on Lake Pichola or Fateh Sagar, where the shimmering reflections of palaces and temples create a magical ambiance. Some lakeside cafes and restaurants also host live music performances, providing a tranquil yet culturally rich evening experience.

Vibrant Bazaars and Night Markets: Rajasthan's lively bazaars and night markets are not just limited to shopping; they also contribute to the state's unique nightlife. Markets like Jaipur's Johari Bazaar and Jodhpur's Sardar Market continue to bustle with activity well into the evening. The vibrant atmosphere, adorned with colorful textiles and handicrafts, offers a different perspective on Rajasthan's cultural vibrancy after sunset.

Camel Safaris by Moonlight: In the desert regions, particularly around Jaisalmer, camel safaris take on a magical quality under the moonlight. Riding through the dunes, with the celestial canopy overhead, provides an otherworldly experience. Some tour operators offer overnight safaris, allowing visitors to camp in the desert and enjoy the tranquility of the night amidst the sand dunes.

Night Photography in Historic Sites: For photography enthusiasts, Rajasthan's historic sites take on a mesmerizing quality at night. The Amber Fort in Jaipur and the City Palace in Udaipur are often open for night photography sessions, allowing visitors to capture the architectural splendor under carefully curated lighting, creating a fusion of history and art.

Conclusion And Further Resources for Planning Your Trip to Rajasthan

Planning a trip to Rajasthan promises a journey into a realm of vibrant culture, rich history, and breathtaking landscapes. From the grandeur of palaces and forts to the tranquility of lakes and deserts, the state offers a diverse tapestry of experiences that captivate the heart and soul of every traveler.

As you embark on your Rajasthan adventure, immerse yourself in the regal ambiance of Jaipur, the romantic allure of Udaipur, the historic tales of Jodhpur, and the cultural richness of Jaisalmer. Explore the lesser-known gems like Bundi, marvel at the architectural wonders of Ranakpur, and experience the spirituality of Pushkar.

Delight your taste buds with the flavors of Rajasthani cuisine, witness traditional art forms and craftsmanship, and participate in the colorful festivities that dot the calendar throughout the year. Whether you choose the bustling markets of Jaipur, the serene dunes of Jaisalmer, or the lush hills of Mount Abu, Rajasthan has something for every type of traveler.

Remember to plan your visit based on the best time to experience the diverse landscapes and cultural events.

Rajasthan's festivals, including the Pushkar Camel Fair and the Jaipur Literature Festival, add an extra layer of vibrancy to your itinerary.

As you explore this majestic state, indulge in outdoor activities, savor local delicacies, and witness the unmatched hospitality of the people. The tales of valor, the melodies of folk music, and the timeless architecture will leave an indelible mark, making your journey through Rajasthan an unforgettable odyssey.

Further Resources for Planning Your Trip:

1. **Tourist Information Centers:**
   - Rajasthan Tourism operates information centers across the state, providing maps, brochures, and assistance for travelers. Visit these centers in major cities for up-to-date information on attractions, accommodations, and transportation.

2. **Official Rajasthan Tourism Website:**
   - The official tourism website of Rajasthan (rajasthantourism.gov.in) is a comprehensive resource for planning your trip. It offers details on destinations, attractions, festivals, and travel itineraries.

3. **Online Travel Forums:**
   - Join online travel forums such as TripAdvisor or Lonely Planet's Thorn Tree for real-time advice from fellow travelers. These platforms are great for gathering tips, recommendations, and firsthand experiences.

4. **Local Experiences and Tours:**
   - Consider booking local experiences and guided tours to enhance your trip. Platforms like Viator and GetYourGuide offer a variety of activities, from heritage walks to desert safaris, allowing you to explore Rajasthan with knowledgeable guides.

5. **Accommodation Booking Platforms:**
   - Use reliable accommodation booking platforms like Booking.com, Airbnb, or Agoda to find a range of options, from luxury heritage hotels to budget-friendly guesthouses. Read reviews to ensure a comfortable stay.

6. **Transportation Booking:**
   - Plan your transportation in advance using platforms like MakeMyTrip, Cleartrip, or the Indian Railways official website for train bookings. For domestic flights, check options on websites like Goibibo or IndiGo.

7. **Language and Cultural Etiquette Guides:**
   - Familiarize yourself with basic Hindi phrases and cultural etiquette to enhance your interactions with locals. Cultural sensitivity is key to fully enjoying your time in Rajasthan.

8. **Weather Apps:**
   - Download weather apps to stay informed about the climate during your visit. Rajasthan experiences extreme temperatures, so planning according to the season is crucial for a comfortable trip.

9. **Health and Safety Precautions:**
   - Prioritize your health and safety by checking travel advisories, getting necessary vaccinations, and carrying a basic first aid kit. Stay hydrated, especially in the desert regions, and follow local guidelines.

By combining these resources with your sense of adventure, Rajasthan will unfold its magic, offering a travel experience that transcends time and leaves you with cherished memories of a journey through the "Land of Kings." Safe travels!

Appendices

Glossary of Local Phrases in Rajasthan

Basic Greetings:

1. **Namaste (नमस्ते):** Hello / Greetings

2. **Sat Sri Akaal (ਸਤਿ ਸ੍ਰੀ ਅਕਾਲ):** Sikh greeting, equivalent to "Hello"

3. **Aap kaise hain? (आप कैसे हैं?):** How are you? (polite)

4. **Shukriya (शुक्रिया):** Thank you

5. **Alvida (अलवदिा):** Goodbye

6. **Phir milenge (फरि मलिंगे):** Until we meet again

Polite Expressions:

7. **Kripaya (कृपया):** Please

8. **Dhanyavaad (धन्यवाद):** Thanks

9. **Koi baat nahi (कोई बात नही):** It's okay / No problem

10. **Mujhe maaf karo (मुझे माफ़ करो)**: Excuse me / I'm sorry

11. **Aapka swagat hai (आपका स्वागत है)**: Welcome (formal)

Getting Around:

12. **Rickshaw kitna hai? (रिक्शा कितना है?)**: How much is the rickshaw fare?

13. **Yeh kahaan hai? (यह कहाँ है?)**: Where is this?

14. **Station / Bus Stand kahan hai? (स्टेशन / बस स्टैंड कहाँ है?)**: Where is the train station / bus stand?

15. **Bazaar kaise jaayenge? (बाज़ार कैसे जाएँगे?)**: How do I get to the market?

Directions:

16. **Right / Left / Straight:**

- **Dahine (दाहिने)**: Right

- **Bayen (बाएँ)**: Left

- **Seedha (सीधा)**: Straight

17. **Peeche mud (पीछे मुड़):** Turn back / U-turn

18. **Yeh kis disha mein hai? (यह किस दिशा में है?):** In which direction is this?

Food and Dining:

19. **Menu dikhaiye (मेनू दिखाइए):** Show me the menu

20. **Yeh kya hai? (यह क्या है?):** What is this?

21. **Aur ek plate (और एक प्लेट):** One more plate

22. **Mithai (मिठाई):** Sweets / Desserts

23. **Chai / Coffee dena (चाय / कॉफ़ी देना):** Serve tea / coffee

24. **Bill laana (बिल लाना):** Bring the bill

Shopping:

25. **Kitne ka hai? (कितने का है?):** How much does it cost?

26. **Mehenga hai (महेंगा है):** It's expensive

27. **Sasta hai (सस्ता है):** It's cheap

28. **Aur dikhao (और दिखाओ):** Show me more

29. **Len-den kahan hota hai? (लेन-देन कहाँ होता है?):** Where is the marketplace?

Numbers:

30. **Ek (एक):** One

31. **Do (दो):** Two

32. **Teen (तीन):** Three

33. **Chaar (चार):** Four

34. **Panch (पाँच):** Five

35. **Das (दस):** Ten

Time and Dates:

36. **Aaj (आज):** Today

37. **Kal (कल):** Tomorrow

38. **Dopahar (दोपहर):** Afternoon

39. **Raat (रात):** Night

40. **Sunday to Saturday:**

- **Ravivaar (रविवार):** Sunday
- **Somvaar (सोमवार):** Monday
- **Mangalvaar (मंगलवार):** Tuesday
- **Budhvaar (बुधवार):** Wednesday
- **Guruvaar (गुरुवार):** Thursday
- **Shukravaar (शुक्रवार):** Friday
- **Shanivaar (शनिवार):** Saturday

Emergencies:

41. **Madad (मदद):** Help

42. **Aag (आग):** Fire

43. **Daktar ko bulao (डॉक्टर को बुलाओ):** Call a doctor

44. **Police ko bulao (पुलिस को बुलाओ):** Call the police

45. **Hospital kahan hai? (हॉस्पटिल कहाँ है?):** Where is the hospital?

Miscellaneous:

46. **Mujhe yeh chahiye (मुझे यह चाहिए):** I need this

47. **Mujhe samajh nahi aaya (मुझे समझ नहीं आया):** I don't understand

48. **Kya aap English bolte hain? (क्या आप इंग्लिश बोलते हैं?):** Do you speak English?

49. **Khuda Hafiz (खुदा हाफ़िज़):** Goodbye (God protect you)

50. **Shubh Ratri (शुभ रात्रि):** Good night

Useful Contacts

Useful Contacts in Rajasthan

Emergency Services:

1. **Police:** 100
   - For reporting crimes, emergencies, or seeking police assistance.

2. **Fire Department:** 101
   - Contact for fire emergencies and rescue operations.

3. **Ambulance:** 108
   - Emergency medical services for swift transportation to hospitals.

Medical Assistance:

4. **Emergency Medical Helpline:** 104
   - Connect with medical professionals for health-related emergencies.

5. **Rajasthan AIDS Control Society Helpline:** 1800-180-1104
   - Information and assistance regarding HIV/AIDS.

6. **Poison Helpline:** 1800-111-555
    - Contact for poisoning emergencies and information.

Tourist Helpline:

7. **Rajasthan Tourism Helpline:** 1800-103-3500
    - Assistance for tourists, travel information, and guidance.

Transportation Services:

8. **Railway Enquiries (IVRS):** 139
    - Indian Railways information and reservation helpline.

9. **Roadways Enquiries:** 0141-2373043
    - Rajasthan State Road Transport Corporation (RSRTC) helpline for bus services.

10. **Airport Enquiries:**
    - **Jaipur International Airport:** 0141-2550623
    - **Jodhpur Airport:** 0291-2512934
    - **Udaipur Airport:** 0294-2655950

Consular Services:

11. **Foreigners Regional Registration Office (FRRO), Jaipur:** 0141-2225624

    o For visa-related assistance and registration for foreign nationals.

Utilities:

12. **Electricity Complaints (Jaipur Vidyut Vitran Nigam Limited):** 1800-180-6507

    o For reporting power outages and electricity-related issues.

13. **Water Supply Complaints:** 1800-180-7080

    o Contact for water supply complaints and information.

Telecom Services:

14. **BSNL Customer Care:** 1500 (Landline/Broadband), 1503 (Mobile)

    o For BSNL telecom services-related queries.

15. **Jio Customer Care:** 1800-88-99999

    o Customer support for Jio telecom services.

Animal Helpline:

16. **RSPCA Helpline (Jaipur):** 0141-2721217

- Rajasthan Society for the Prevention of Cruelty to Animals.

Women's Helpline:

17. **Women Helpline (Rajasthan):** 1090

    - Assistance and support for women in distress.

Child Helpline:

18. **Child Helpline (Rajasthan):** 1098

    - Assistance for child protection and welfare.

Legal Aid:

19. **Rajasthan State Legal Services Authority:** 1800-180-6127

    - Legal aid and assistance for those in need.

Environment Helpline:

20. **Rajasthan State Pollution Control Board Helpline:** 0141-2227842

    - Environmental assistance and pollution-related complaints.

Sample Itineraries

Sample Itinerary 1: "Golden Triangle and Beyond"

Duration: 7 Days

Day 1: Arrival in Delhi

- Arrive in Delhi, India's capital.
- Visit India Gate and explore the vibrant markets of Connaught Place.
- Overnight stay in Delhi.

Day 2: Delhi Sightseeing

- Explore historic landmarks: Red Fort, Jama Masjid, and Raj Ghat.
- Visit Humayun's Tomb and Qutub Minar.
- Discover the bustling lanes of Chandni Chowk.
- Overnight stay in Delhi.

Day 3: Agra - The City of Taj

- Travel to Agra.
- Visit the iconic Taj Mahal, Agra Fort, and Mehtab Bagh.
- Explore local markets.

- Overnight stay in Agra.

Day 4: Jaipur - The Pink City

- Drive to Jaipur, the Pink City.
- Visit Amber Fort, Hawa Mahal, and City Palace.
- Explore the local markets.
- Overnight stay in Jaipur.

Day 5: Jaipur Sightseeing

- Explore Jantar Mantar and Albert Hall Museum.
- Visit Jal Mahal and Nahargarh Fort.
- Experience the cultural charm at Chokhi Dhani.
- Overnight stay in Jaipur.

Day 6: Pushkar

- Drive to Pushkar.
- Visit the holy Pushkar Lake and Brahma Temple.
- Explore the vibrant bazaars.
- Overnight stay in Pushkar.

Day 7: Departure from Jaipur

- Return to Jaipur for departure.

- Optional: Visit the City Palace or other missed attractions.
- Depart from Jaipur.

Sample Itinerary 2: "Desert Delight"

Duration: 10 Days

Day 1-2: Arrival in Jodhpur

- Arrive in Jodhpur, the Blue City.
- Explore Mehrangarh Fort and Jaswant Thada.
- Stroll through the vibrant streets of the old town.
- Overnight stay in Jodhpur.

Day 3-4: Jaisalmer - The Golden City

- Drive to Jaisalmer.
- Explore Jaisalmer Fort, Patwon Ki Haveli, and Gadisar Lake.
- Experience a camel safari in the Thar Desert.
- Overnight stay in a desert camp.

Day 5-6: Bikaner

- Drive to Bikaner.
- Visit Junagarh Fort and Karni Mata Temple.

- Explore the colorful streets of the old city.
- Overnight stay in Bikaner.

Day 7-8: Shekhawati Region

- Explore the painted havelis of Mandawa and Nawalgarh.
- Witness the artistic heritage of the region.
- Overnight stay in a heritage hotel.

Day 9-10: Return to Jaipur

- Return to Jaipur.
- Visit the City Palace, Hawa Mahal, and Jantar Mantar.
- Explore local markets for shopping.
- Depart from Jaipur.

Sample Itinerary 3: "Cultural Extravaganza"

Duration: 14 Days

Day 1-3: Arrival in Udaipur

- Arrive in Udaipur, the City of Lakes.
- Explore City Palace, Jag Mandir, and Jagdish Temple.

- Boat ride on Lake Pichola.
- Overnight stay in Udaipur.

Day 4-5: Mount Abu

- Drive to Mount Abu, the only hill station in Rajasthan.
- Visit Dilwara Jain Temples and Nakki Lake.
- Explore the serene landscapes.
- Overnight stay in Mount Abu.

Day 6-8: Ranthambore National Park

- Travel to Ranthambore.
- Go on safaris to spot tigers and wildlife.
- Explore Ranthambore Fort.
- Overnight stays in Ranthambore.

Day 9-10: Bundi

- Drive to Bundi.
- Visit Taragarh Fort, Bundi Palace, and Chitrashala.
- Explore the step wells and local markets.
- Overnight stay in Bundi.

Day 11-14: Jaipur

- Drive to Jaipur.
- Explore Amer Fort, City Palace, and Hawa Mahal.
- Visit local markets and indulge in Rajasthani cuisine.
- Attend a cultural show or workshop.
- Depart from Jaipur.

These itineraries provide a blend of historical exploration, cultural experiences, and natural beauty, allowing you to immerse yourself in the diverse tapestry of Rajasthan.

Packing Checklist

Rajasthan Trip Packing Checklist

1. Clothing:

- Lightweight and breathable clothing for daytime exploration.
- Modest clothing for visits to temples and religious sites.
- Comfortable walking shoes for city tours and sightseeing.
- Sandals or flip-flops for relaxed evenings.
- Hat or cap for sun protection.
- Scarf or shawl for covering shoulders when needed.
- Warm layers for cooler evenings, especially during winter.

2. Travel Essentials:

- Passport, visa, and necessary travel documents.
- Printed or electronic copies of hotel reservations and itinerary.
- Travel insurance details.

- Personal identification (ID) and photocopies.
- Credit/debit cards and some local currency.

3. Health and Personal Care:

- Prescription medications and a copy of the prescription.
- Basic first aid kit (band-aids, pain relievers, antiseptic).
- Insect repellent.
- Sunscreen with high SPF.
- Personal hygiene items (toothbrush, toothpaste, etc.).
- Hand sanitizer.

4. Electronics:

- Mobile phone and charger.
- Camera or smartphone for photos.
- Power bank for charging devices on the go.
- Adapters for charging electronics (if necessary).

5. Travel Accessories:

- Lightweight daypack for daily excursions.
- Travel pillow for long journeys.

- Sunglasses.
- Travel guidebook or maps.

6. Miscellaneous:

- Snacks and reusable water bottle.
- Travel umbrella or rain jacket.
- Multi-tool or pocketknife.
- Zip-lock bags for organizing items.
- Travel laundry detergent for longer trips.
- Extra set of keys.
- Journal and pen for documenting your journey.

7. Clothing for Special Activities:

- Swimwear for hotel pools or water activities.
- Comfortable clothes for camel rides or outdoor adventures.

8. Optional Items:

- Binoculars for wildlife safaris.
- Power strip for charging multiple devices.
- Travel lock for securing luggage.
- Books or e-reader for leisure reading.

9. Seasonal Considerations:

- During winter (November to February), pack warmer clothing, especially for nights.
- In the summer months (March to June), lightweight and cool fabrics are essential.

10. Local Shopping:

- Leave some space in your suitcase for traditional Rajasthani attire or handicrafts you might purchase during your trip.

Remember to check the weather forecast for your specific travel dates and destinations within Rajasthan. Adjust the list based on your personal preferences and the nature of your planned activities.

Safe Travels!

Printed in Great Britain
by Amazon